Learn to Sing to Learn Read

a course book for parents and teachers
by **Audrey Wisbey** with Janet Thomas

British Broadcasting Corporation

D0510839

Published by the British Broadcasting Corporation
35 Marylebone High Street
London W1M 4AA

ISBN 0 563 17640 7

Typeset by The Yale Press Ltd, London, SE25

Printed and bound by Mackays of Chatham Ltd

CONTENTS

INTRODUCTION

Every day I am finding normal intelligent children who have failed to learn to read. They often have difficulty in singing in tune, do not use their eyes together very well and appear to be somewhat clumsy.

Studying these children I find the trouble frequently appears to stem from undetected hearing problems during very early childhood, particularly in the first year; the kind of problem that comes with the common cold, respiratory infections, middle ear difficulties, enlarged adenoids and a great variety of conditions that are fairly common in early childhood. This means that sound would often appear to be a low, dull noise to the child, thus preventing it from becoming interested in sound or learning all the variety of sound ingredients that go together to make up the speech sound. These ingredients are the musical pitch and tonal qualities of the speech sounds, how long they last and their variations in loudness levels. The accurate blending together of these ingredients requires the ability to hear very small changes in each of them and also requires great sensitivity of hearing accompanied by plenty of practice.

Learning to speak in the usual way is dependent upon hearing all the sounds to be copied, sufficiently often and consistently. These sounds to be copied are all the components or ingredients of speech which can eventually be blended together to make the various speech sounds and stored away in the memory for reference purposes when at a later stage they can be used in trying to immediately recognise the speech of others. The child's sensitive ear can be trained to recognise the very fine changes in musical pitch that occur as one speech sound is joined to another by the speech organs gradually making the appropriate movements and so changing their shape. In this way the exact recognition and reproduction of speech sounds that is the forerunner of good spelling and language patterns is made possible.

Children appear to learn one sound at a time as a result of a massive amount of listening and experimental vocalisation. Research suggests that a year's experience of this continued repetition is necessary for the firm establishment of the memory of the sounds' components. The sound that most children seem to learn first is that of middle 'C', possibly because the work of many suggests that our language has a tonal centre of 'C'. Initially, middle 'C' appears to be the lowest note that young children can produce with any degree of control, just as 'G' is the highest note capable of being produced with the sustained control needed for singing in tune, but as control develops so their range increases. Children in the first few years of life appear to be able to hear and so learn the exact pitch and tonal quality of each sound, recognising the slightest variation in either. This ability extends to a slightly lesser degree to the hearing for loudness levels and duration patterns. Unfortunately, this ability very quickly begins to fade and as early as six years of age the hearing for the highest pitched sounds is diminishing and becomes insufficient for first learning. Fortunately, once learnt, providing memory has been firmly established, little hearing is required to reinforce the learning and so the remembrance of the sound. This does therefore make both the building up of the memory of sounds, and the checking that the hearing is sufficiently acute for this, vitally important.

Other research has shown that the constant babbling or experimental vocalisation of the very young child is aiding the learning of the sounds so vocalised, providing the hearing of the child is normal. It has also been shown, however, that children could be learning just the sensation of vocalising called 'the kinaesthetic sensation of speech' if their hearing is not consistently reliable. This could mean that although the child is speaking, it is not building up an Auditory Memory and this may not be discovered until the child is required to use this memory in such skills as Reading, Spelling or singing intervals in tune. By then the natural fading or hearing for high pitched sounds could mean that there is difficulty in making good this lack of memory. After all, how do you learn a sound for the first time if you cannot hear the sound?

Consistently reliable hearing is therefore vital. What makes hearing inconsistent and unreliable? Many childhood ailments can be the cause of this, the results of which are unseen! Childhood catarrh, sinusitis, tonsillitis, respiratory infections, enlarged adenoids, glue ear are among the culprits. Middle ear problems, causing variations in the quality and dulling the reception of the sounds heard, can be unseen and are very common during babyhood, particularly during the first year of life. It is not surprising therefore that so many children with reading problems are found to have suffered many episodes of middle ear disorders in babyhood, when the most minimal hearing loss has such catastrophic consequences on language development. Continued problems can be detected by the use of suitable hearing tests but many of these conditions are variable. Unfortunately, children tend to be tested only when they are reasonably free of these conditions. Perhaps this is because the condition causing the difficulty requires the child to be kept in a warm temperature at home and erring on the side of safety the child is kept at home for suitable periods after the acute stage has been cleared up before taking him to have his hearing tested. Even then the hearing test is only describing the hearing as it was at the time of testing. To learn, the child must hear and have sounds to hear regularly and consistently. How can a parent ensure that this is happening to their child? There is only one way and that is to regularly and consistently involve the child in suitable sound making activities. These must be enjoyable, yet provide the learning required for the language skills in a logical, one sound at a time approach, and also give daily information about the child's hearing. For this reason, a Record Book with daily details of the child's response to sounds and the learning of them should be regularly and carefully maintained. Suitable activities *must* be musical, because it is only this type of activity that allows the child to experience and so learn all the auditory ingredients of language, one at a time, in a logical, progressive manner. The simplest speech sound is a complex mixture of all the ingredients of Pitch, Tonal Quality, Loudness and Duration Variation. Does it not make sense to ensure that the child has the chance to learn these, one at a time, by continually checking that the hearing is normal and then providing the continuous experience in order to learn at the time of day when he can learn most efficiently and in a manner most suitable for learning? This 'time of the day' is early in the morning when the hearing is most acute and 'in a manner most suitable' means keeping the activity fun and the sessions short. Fatigue sets in quickly with young children and a fatigued ear distorts the pitch of the sounds heard thus causing confusion instead of learning.

The recognition of the speech of others requires the ability to immediately analyse and identify through the hearing system the auditory ingredients of each speech sound used. This requires the memory arising from the previous learning which should have taken place during the early years.

These are the years when the hearing sensitivity, already described, normally co-exists with a great receptive and malleable condition of the brain to make the learning of all important and interesting new sounds possible. At the same time it exists for other forms of learning such as the ability to hear the differences in pitch and tone of each sound thus identifying it and so learning to distinguish the important sounds from the unimportant. The slightest variations in pitch, loudness levels and durations, can also be learnt in order correctly to localise the sound sources, judge their distances, direction and speed of travel. All of this is necessary for both self preservation and spatial awareness.

This ability is also required to 'trigger off' the visual development of the child. The child may be born with perfectly good eyes held in position by six muscles, but unless the eye muscles are exercised by use to make it possible to turn those little tunnels of good vision quickly and efficiently in the correct direction, the child's visual development will be immature and learning will be hampered. The baby's accurate visual localising of a sound source and attempts to slowly pursue these sources when they are interesting and important, such as the approach of 'Mum' or food, provides much of the essential practice. Correct localising of sounds requires the ability to hear equally well in both ears as well as the small changes of pitch and loudness levels that are involved in moving sound sources. (Next time a car approaches and passes your house listen with your eyes closed to help you realise how much you can recognise as regards distance, direction and speed of travel, through your hearing). If a child cannot correctly localise a sound because a slight hearing loss in one ear appears to alter the direction of the sound, then soon he will give up attempting to seek out the sound source. Reduced hearing levels making sound lose its impact or interest will also reduce these attempts and so essential opportunities to use the eye muscles and so gain control and co-ordination will be lost.

The ability to pull the eyes together at varying positions in space is similar to being able to focus a camera on objects of different distances and sizes and to maintain that focus. Good vision requires this ability. Visual Memory requires good vision also to be available when the brain is most fertile. Learning to read involves the recognition of the previously learnt visual symbols that codify previously learnt speech sounds.

Musical games providing the pre-reading experience for children that the endless playing with toys, modelling clay, drawing books and so on provides for the visual system are therefore essential. As already explained, how else but in music can one take each of the sound ingredients individually and play with them? The child learns shape, form, colour, hand/eye co-ordination etc., by playing with toys long before it is expected to cope with the task of recognising and learning the printed word. Why can it not have the chance to build its memory of the musical pitch, tonal quality, duration and intensity patterns involved in language, similarly through games? The child can neither blend together sounds that it has never heard, nor recognise their visual symbol. The involvement of the child in suitable games will take advantage of the greater learning made possible by active participation. Sounds seem to be heard louder by a child if he makes the sounds for himself and of course if he is taught to do this he will not be so dependent on adults to provide the sounds for him to learn. Care must be taken to ensure that the sounds available for learning include all those needed and that they are accurate. Some hearing problems cause distortion of the sound being received; this distortion will therefore be learnt. Games involving pitch discrimination will identify these problems. The regular provision of the softest level of sound that can be heard by the child will ensure that the most accurate sensation of pitch will be experienced and so learnt. For this reason tuning and playing on the tone bars of the xylophone should be carried out very softly. Humming is an effective method of ensuring a good quality of sound and preventing shouting.

This is an important aspect of learning through hearing. We forget that as sounds by nature are transient and ephemeral they do not just 'sit in space' before us for our continued learning in the way that visual objects do so very conveniently. No wonder that in spite of hearing being so fully developed at birth (and even before that) and vision taking several months to develop sufficient muscular control necessary for reasonably efficient use, the visual system gradually takes over while the hearing system tends to become daily more lazy and inefficient. Opportunities, together with the need to use our hearing, are therefore essential if potential is to be achieved.

Meaning is another aspect of learning that is seriously misunderstood. If the meaning of a sound is not initially demonstrated in association with a sound source, such as a dog actually seen and heard to be barking, how will a child at a later date be able to correctly identify the sound of barking? Unlike vision, we cannot collect the meaning of a sound through our hearing simultaneously with the hearing of the sound. This must be collected via our other senses and so it must be demonstrated simultaneously with the sound presentation. Can we remember meaningless sounds? Try listening to a completely strange language. You may hear it very well but can you later remember the sounds involved? If a child cannot collect the meaning of a sound he may well be in a similar position. The opportunity to collect the meaning of the sounds and constantly reinforce this, arises from the opportunities provided by the environment and much multi-sensory experience, particularly the visual and motor systems operating efficiently during early childhood. If meaning cannot be collected because of a visual problem or physical handicap then Auditory Memory will be hampered in its development, unless alternative opportunities are made available as soon as possible.

Playing these games with young children will mean that you are sure they are learning them, or at least any difficulties will be brought to your attention. Early medical attention can then be sought. Do not wait for a child to fail in the classroom before finding out whether he has or has had a problem. You can never give a child back that early childhood period of sensory acuity. The added bonus following these games will be that the child will become musically literate, a state that is justified on its own merits for educational, cultural and recreational reasons. This means of course that even if the child is thought not to have any problems no time will have been wasted.

The urgency of the problem? I have found that something like 55% of the school population appear to have had hearing problems at some stage or other which could have prevented them from achieving their true potential in literacy efficiency.

HOW TO USE THIS BOOK

This is a course-book, primarily intended to cover the basic training necessary for the development of Auditory Memory, as an essential element in the learning of language and literacy.

The material of the Course is introduced in logical sequence, with advice on how it should be applied and why it is useful. Though it is geared for the pre-school child it could be adapted for older ones. It is based on the way a child's hearing functions.

It is addressed to parents, teachers and workers with children. Though designed for one child at a time, it is equally suitable for use in the classroom. It assumes no previous knowledge of music on the part of the adults who will use it.

The arrangement of the book is in steps, subdivided into eight stages. Initially it is envisaged that a step will take about five minutes to complete; but as progress is made this will increase to about twenty minutes. 'Little, but often' is a very good maxim: but, though the hearing training should be carried out in short sessions, the supporting activities can take place at any time during the day, and may last as long as you wish. If a child can perform the activities immediately, that does *not* mean he need not carry on. What it does mean is that you must exercise all your ingenuity to keep alive the child's interest during many repetitions. Performance is but the starting point: much repetition of the experiences is needed, over a period of about a year, before memory is really established. It is therefore advisable never to work through more than one step in a day, regardless of how much time is spent on the full range of follow-on activities. To proceed too quickly without adequate repetition will not help develop memory and, as most literacy skills are memory-dependent, much time will be lost. Many children who initially can perform the activities satisfactorily later fail if they have never had the opportunity for consistent repetition.

The aim should be to repeat as many of the steps in the book as often as possible (without boredom), and to move on as slowly as possible. Every child hears slightly differently, so do not expect a uniform reaction to all parts of the course by the same or by different children. There is one positive advantage in doing the course with several children at once: as each child attempts individual tasks there will be the maximum of repetition with the minimum of boredom. (For example, the game of 'Hunt the Toffee' in step 18. Each child in turn can try to find the toffee while the other children make the sounds.)

The brain of the pre-six-year-old child grows so quickly that forgetting is just as easy as learning. It is for this reason that so much repetition, over such a long period, is essential. And this, too, is why every session should gradually become what we call a Learning Sandwich, adopting a pattern whereby you (i) introduce new material, (ii) revise old material, and (iii) revise new material, relating it to the old.

Do not miss anything out. You may feel that some of the activities are merely for fun, and so can be excluded from a busy learning programme. I hope that all are fun; but please remember that there is a reason for every activity. Literacy arises from the combined memorising of *all* sensory experiences.

Carefully keep a Record Book of how each child performs each activity, and of how long it takes for each child to become proficient in each activity. Underline in red if a child continuously fails to perform satisfactorily at any point. It is very important to record variations in a child's response to sound, as the busy doctor often picks up a failure only if it is present at the time of examination. The worst problems in literacy seem to arise when a child has a *variable* problem, which can range from reasonably normal hearing to varying degrees of deafness. When a child continues to fail after a month's work then ask that he be seen by an Ear, Nose and Throat specialist and an Audiologist and send along a copy of the record you have kept.

Growing children need adequate exercise of their eye muscles if they are to have the opportunity to learn such information as space, distance and direction. Musical sounds can be used to aid this development, through visits to the railway station, watching cars come and go, putting the musical train in the tunnel (page 00), dancing to music and so forth. You should not underestimate the importance of such activities. Similarly, movement control and co-ordination need for their learning much practice – in moving to sounds, in refocusing the eyes following movement of the body and so on. Many clumsy children appear to suffer simply from a deficient experience in developing *memory* of the movements needed for control and co-ordination.

Each Stage introduces a new sound. It may be that a child can cope with the work on one note but not on another. Note this on the Record Book. It is the very first note that will probably take the longest time to learn.

Home-made badges, to be awarded at the end of each Stage, and the use of Test Cards are fun for the child; and they also assist in the keeping of records.

Before you begin
Study the Introduction carefully. Read quickly through the book, to gain an overall picture of how the method works. Study each Stage to ensure that you have available the equipment needed.

A suitable Instrument
A Xylophone or Glockenspiel will be required. These are relatively inexpensive and are readily available. Do not buy cheap or 'toy' instruments, because these are often tuned incorrectly.

The following makes are recommended: 'New Era', 'Granton' and 'Suzuki' *Diatonic* Soprano or Contralto Xylophones. The Tone Bars of the instruments must be removable – this is essential. Ideally the range should be from middle C to top F (cost range £22 to £37). As an alternative, instruments may be hired at a cost of about 50p per week from C. Foote, Golden Square, London W1. Soft, but not woolly-headed, beaters produce the best sound for this type of work. Later on, home-made instruments can be made. Access to a piano is also helpful, but not absolutely essential.

A recording is available, which gives examples of the various games when it is thought that this could be a useful addition.

Please feel free at any time to contact me about individual problems or unusual problems, but in so doing will you please enclose a stamped addressed envelope.

STAGE ONE

Step 1 Introducing the musical instrument and 'musical ladder'

Keep the sessions short and fun and hold them early in the day. Don't forget to praise and encourage the child. Start your record book (see Introduction, page 00)

A xylophone (or similar instrument) is like a musical ladder. You can move 'up' and 'down' it from 'top' to 'bottom', one or more steps at a time, and it has 'high' and 'low' notes. An understanding of these concepts is important for later pitch discrimination. You should therefore make sure the child understands the shape and form of a ladder, by demonstrating on a ladder, steps or flights of stairs and by searching in books and magazines for pictures of ladders being used.

Encourage the child to copy you in climbing up and down the first two or three steps of a ladder or stairs. When the function of a ladder is clearly understood, explain that a 'musical ladder' is used for climbing up and down sounds.

Get out the xylophone and sit next to the child, with the longest tone bar nearest to you both.

Point out that the xylophone looks like a ladder, and that each tone bar is like a rung or step. Notice that each bar has a letter-name engraved on it.

With a soft-headed beater, play each tone bar in turn, from the lowest note (longest bar) to the highest note and back again. Play gently and softly in the middle of the tone bar to produce a good quality sound.

Ask the child to 'climb up and down the sounds' in the same way.

Make sure he understands the connection between the 'musical' and ordinary ladder by asking him to climb up a step on the ladder or stairs for every 'step' you climb on the xylophone.

Help the child to draw a ladder. Point to each step of the picture-ladder and ask him to play the correct step on the musical ladder (the xylophone).

Reverse this procedure: you play when the child points.

This is probably enough for one day. Stop while it is still fun for the child, so that he looks forward to the next session.

Relevant activities such as climbing 'up' and 'down' the stairs will reinforce meaning and so aid learning. The act of drawing provides valuable hand/eye training.

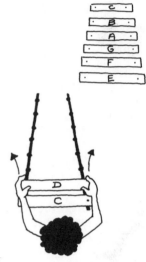

Step 2   Finding the first note to be learnt: middle C

Sounds are learnt one at a time after much repetition.

Middle C is the easiest note for most children to learn. Reducing the xylophone to a one-rung musical ladder ensures that the child gets plenty of experience of middle C without being distracted by the other notes.

Check that Step 1 has been clearly understood and remembered before moving on.

Ask the child to play the bottom and lowest sound on his musical ladder – softly – in the middle of the tone bar. Point out that this bar has the letter-name 'C' engraved on it.

Teach the child how to remove all the tone bars except this 'C', by holding each bar at both ends and lifting it carefully upwards and off the pins. Encourage him to name each bar as he removes it.

Ask the child to draw a ladder looking just like the xylophone with only one rung at the bottom. Ask him to play the 'musical step' C softly each time you point to the rung on the picture ladder.

Reverse this procedure: you play when the child points.

Liken the lowest step to the lowest part of the body, the toes, and ask the child to touch his toes when you play the C tone bar -softly.

Carry the xylophone around the house to find other objects that make C sounds when tapped or moved (e.g. cups, bottles with some liquid in, squeaky hinges, doorbells). For the moment, don't worry if the C sounds are higher or lower than your xylophone's C.

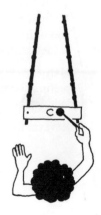

Stop while it is still fun, and ask the child to put the tone bars back on the xylophone.

Children, like adults, learn things by doing them themselves. It is important to play C softly, since the pitch sensation will be experienced more accurately the softer the sound.

14

Step 3 Tuning the voice to the instrument and introducing practice

Keep the sessions short and fun, and hold them early in the day.

'Tuning' the voice, by humming very softly the same sound that is being played softly on the xylophone, is one way of developing an understanding of what is meant by listening. If a child vocalises a sound, it helps him to learn it. Most children can hum in tune before they can sing in tune. Humming also produces a good quality sound, with warmth and resonance, and makes it impossible to shout.

Practising is an important part of the programme, since it provides not only more repetition of C but also gives scope for the gradual development of the self-discipline through which a child learns to organise his own time.

Ask the child to remove all the tone bars except the C, as he has been taught. Remind him of the one-rung musical ladder.

Explain to the child that musicians always 'tune' their instruments at the beginning of a concert to make sure they make a pleasant sound when they play together. In the same way you and the child are going to learn to 'tune your voices' to the xylophone to make sure they make a pleasant sound.

Demonstrate how to 'tune' the voice, by playing softly in the middle of the tone bar and humming the same sound very softly. Ask the child to copy you. Explain that he must be able to hear his soft playing while he is humming, and that both sounds should be the same.

Ask the child what sort of animal or insect makes a humming sound. If his answer is not appropriate, suggest a bee, and help him draw and colour a small one on a piece of card, and then cut it out.

Ask the child to tune his voice whenever you sit the bee on the C rung of the ladder. (Keep this bee in a safe place for future use!)

Explain to the child that all musicians practise, both to improve their playing and so that they will not forget what they have already learnt. Ask him to practise tuning for just a minute or two every day, on his own. Tell him you will be practising too, and ask him to show you what he will be practising, to make sure that he understands.

Remind the child to put the tone bars back on the xylophone after each learning and practice session.

In future, tuning will be done at the start of every session and frequently during it, as well as at practice time. Practice sessions should be regular and short – at this stage no more than one or two minutes daily. Do not hover over the child while he is practising, but do keep a 'watchful ear' on what he is doing. Show him you consider it important by asking each day whether he has done his practice, and be seen and heard to practise yourself.

Step 4   Learning to listen

Accurate copying of sounds needs careful listening

The child may not yet know what is meant by 'listening': he must experience it before he can understand what it means. Listening involves attention to sound. To ensure that a child is listening he must be engaged in activities that require a response to what he has heard. Unless a child learns to listen carefully, he will not copy, and therefore learn, sounds accurately.

> With only the C tone bar on the xylophone, first tune your voice, and then ask the child to do the same. Ask the child if he remembered his practice, and tell him when you did yours.
>
> Demonstrate soft humming to match the sound played, telling the child to listen to the sounds you are making. Use the word 'listen' frequently during this step.
>
> Ask the child to play the sound, listen very carefully and then copy the sound by humming.
>
> Ask the child to close his eyes and to listen carefully for the moment at which he first hears you playing the tone bar, then open his eyes and play the sound himself. (Play very softly in the middle of the bar.)
>
> Ask the child to close his eyes again and listen to the softest sounds he can hear (e.g. clock ticking, cars passing, birds singing, footsteps).

It is often a good idea to precede the tuning at the start of each session with listening to the softest sounds that can be heard. This will help the development of listening and discrimination.

From now on, steps will often include some follow-on activities which will enhance the learning sessions, are extra fun and can be carried out later in the day, sometimes on walks or excursions. *These activities are part of the programme and not optional extras.*

Follow-on activities

1   If you have or can borrow a tape recorder (an inexpensive cassette recorder is fine), recording environmental sounds with the child will develop his interest in sound, and the recordings can be used for training the memory and developing discrimination.

Show the child how the tape recorder can record and play back sounds picked up by its microphone, and take him with you to record sounds from your local environment – animals, cars, buses, children's playground noises and so on. Make sure the child observes you recording.

At home, let the child identify the sounds you have recorded together. At story time, make up stories around the sounds, playing them at the right moment in the story. If you are not very good at making up stories, you can look at children's story books *before* going out to collect sound effects with the child, so that you can collect appropriate ones.

2   Prepare a tray of scraps of different material (rough, silky, furry and so on) for the child to touch and identify when blindfolded.

3   Repeat with objects to be tasted.

4   Repeat with objects to be smelt.

Meaningless sounds are not easily remembered. As a child collects the meaning of sounds through activities involving all his senses – seeing, smelling, touching and even tasting – give him some practice to make sure they are all working well.

Step 5   Loud and soft sounds

The aim is to move on as slowly as possible, so some steps may take several days to complete. Keep the record book daily.

The idea of soft and loud sounds can be taught by using the xylophone (reduced to tone bar middle C) with a variety of hard and soft beaters which will give a wide range of sound qualities. As well as encouraging the development of the child's listening and discrimination, this will *eventually* give valuable information about his hearing, if the record book is kept regularly.

Working with closed eyes makes the child use his ears

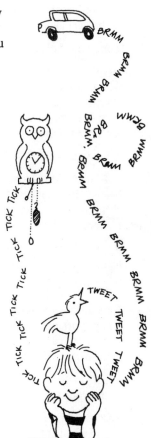

instead of relying on visual clues; but before doing this he must be allowed first to collect information about the new sounds through all his senses. Only thus will the sounds acquire a meaning for him, making it easier to memorise them. Memory *span*, which is all-important, will be developed through copying *patterns* of these learnt sounds.

Both you and the child tune your voices.

Using the soft-headed beater, demonstrate both loud and soft sounds on the C tone bar, and make sure the child understands what is meant by both. Let him see the bigger action of loud playing compared with the smaller one of soft playing, and use the words 'loud' and 'soft' freely in your demonstration.

Tune your voices.

Encourage the child to copy your actions and produce loud and soft sounds, using every degree possible from the very, very soft to the very, very loud, in random order one at a time.

Tune your voices.

Help the children to make a variety of beaters (with heads of wood, metal, cork, wool, sponge, etc.), and then explore the varying softness and loudness of the sounds that can be made with each of them, as well as with the hard-headed beater that comes with the xylophone.

Tune your voices.

Ask the child to close his eyes, and with the original soft-headed beater play a loud sound in the middle of the tone bar. Ask the child to open his eyes and play the same kind of sound you played.

Repeat, exploring the fullest possible range of loud and soft levels. Make sure the child listens with his eyes closed.

Tune your voices.

Repeat these activities using all your beaters. Choose the beater to be used *after* the child has closed his eyes, so that he has to listen even more carefully to the quality of sound in order to select the right beater. Extend the child's vocabulary by describing the sounds – woolly, harsh, and so on.

Tune your voices.

Ask the child to close his eyes and listen, then play two sounds, one after the other. For this you can use the same beater, or different beaters for each sound, and the sounds may be of either the same or different loudness. Ask the child to open his eyes and copy you. Repeat several times with a variety of beaters and degrees of loudness, for example:

First beat	Second beat
very loud (wood)	soft (wood)
loud (metal)	soft (cork)
soft (metal)	loud (sponge)

Tune your voices.

When the child can accurately copy patterns of two sounds, gradually extend the number one by one. Do not move on too quickly, as this will lead to careless listening.

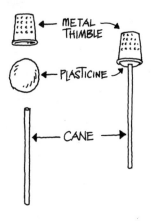

About a year's repeated listening and repetition is needed before a sound is accurately remembered. Since the child's hearing and performance will vary from day to day, it is important to keep your record book regularly. From it you will be able to spot any consistent difficulties that recur over a long period.

Step 6 The importance of importance

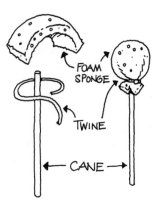

Parents and teachers are the centre of the young child's world. What they show to be of importance will be learnt as important.

The xylophone with its C tone bar and a variety of beaters can be used as a sound detector. By carrying them around the home or school and searching out sounds that match, the child continues to learn the pitched sound of C, while also learning to discriminate between the sounds of his environment (sounds which contribute to his knowledge of it). His parent's or teacher's involvement in the activity shows him its importance. Seeking out objects with the eyes gives the muscles valuable exercise. This ability develops as a result of the recognition of the sounds involved in movement and direction.

Tune your voices.

Play 'I Spy' with the child in the kitchen, choosing objects different distances away from him.

Tune your voices.

Taking xylophone and beaters, explore the kitchen with the child, searching for sounds that match the xylophone's C when they are struck, blown, rubbed, scraped or rattled. (Do not worry if these Cs are higher or lower than the one on your xylophone.)

Tune your voices.

With one beater, play the various sounds of C you have

discovered in a variety of short patterns, such as:

    loud, loud, soft, soft, loud

    loud, soft, soft, loud, soft, soft

Let the child copy each pattern.

Tune your voices.

Repeat the patterns with the child playing on the kitchen utensils and you playing on the xylophone with whichever beater most accurately matches each sound the child is making. If you have a tape recorder, record these efforts. At later listening, ask the child to identify the objects played.

Tune your voices.

Suggest to the child that you use the xylophone as a dinner gong to bring the whole family to the table. Demonstrate by taking the xylophone to the table and asking the child to sit down when you play on C.

The action of sitting down will reinforce the idea of a lowish-pitched note – and the connection with meals will soon show middle C to be very important!

Attitude to an activity is learnt. If you develop the habit of humming the note C while you are waiting for the kettle to boil or a cake to bake, and can be seen to allocate time for the music session and practice, the child will learn by observation to accept the importance of these activities.

Follow-on Activities

Repeat all the activities in this step in and out of the home. Explore the bathroom, living room and bedrooms before going out of doors.

Record 'tunes' made up in each one and name them 'Bathroom Symphony in C', 'Bedroom Rhapsody in C', 'Garden Overture' and so on. Listen to them later and identify the objects played. 'Tunes' at this stage just means playing on different objects.

All pitched sounds contribute to the child's learning about his world.

Playing 'I Spy' provides valuable and necessary exercise for the eye muscles.

These are not optional extras.

Step 7   Bright and dull sounds

The most exact copying of sounds and their qualities will lead to accurate discrimination.

The range of sounds obtainable on the C tone bar with a variety of beaters can be extended by using the players' hands to dampen the sound so as to reduce the overtones. This is an effective way of eventually obtaining information about the child's hearing for high pitched sounds, and it will make a useful contribution to the record book.

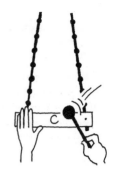

> Listen to and name the softest sounds you can both hear around you.
>
> Tune your voices.
>
> With the soft-headed beater, play a fairly loud sound in the middle of the tone bar.
>
> Place your hand on the end of the tone bar and play another fairly loud sound. Point out to the child how much duller this is than when you are not touching the tone bar. Demonstrate the difference between the dull and bright sound while the child watches.

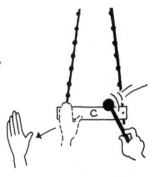

> Tune your voices.
>
> Encourage the child to copy your actions and make first dull and then bright sounds. Let him explore dull and bright sounds with the whole variety of beaters and encourage him to describe the sounds he makes.

> Tune your voices.
>
> Ask the child to close his eyes while you play dull or bright sounds with a variety of beaters. After each one, tell him to open his eyes and make the same sound.
>
> Tune your voices.
>
> Ask the child to close his eyes and tell him you will play patterns of first bright and then dull sounds. Explain that he should keep his eyes closed, but shoot up his hand as soon as he hears the sound change from bright to dull. Use a different beater for each pattern.
>
> Tune your voices.
>
> Reverse this process: you close your eyes while the child plays
>
> Tune your voices

Since all the activities in Stage One are on Middle C, from now on the note will not normally be specified; but remember all singing, as well as playing should be on this note.

Step 8   Fast- and slow-moving sounds

Do not miss anything out – there is a reason for every activity.

The speech sounds that must be recognised when learning to read are made up of pitched sounds, blended together as musical chords and moving at various speeds. Music that suggests quick or slow movement can be used to develop discrimination between fast- and slow-moving sounds; moving to the music reinforces the meaning which is essential for learning, as well as developing the self-control that comes from practice in handling stimulation through all the senses.

Tune your voices.

Ask the child to run around while you play the tone bar but 'freeze' like a statue whenever you stop.

Tune your voices.

If recorded music is available, choose some which suggests slow walking. Play this and ask the child to walk slowly round the room matching his movement to the music. Use the word 'slow' frequently.

Tune your voices.

Using music that suggests running movement, ask the child to run in time to the music. Explain that he is running quickly.

Tune your voices.

With the child, watch cars, bicycles and pedestrians go past the house and jointly decide whether they are moving slowly, quickly, very slowly or very quickly, and so on. Play with the child's toys, moving them slowly or quickly.

Tune your voices.

Explain to the child that when you play quick-moving sounds on the xylophone he must move quickly in time to your playing. Demonstrate playing quick-moving sounds while he watches, then ask him to move in time to them.

Repeat with slow-moving sounds.

Tune your voices.

Ask the child to close his eyes while you play slow- or quick-moving sounds. When you finish he must open his eyes and play the same speed of sounds.

Tune your voices.

Play patterns of quick and slow sounds for the child to listen to

with his eyes closed. Ask him to open his eyes and copy the
sounds, for example:
    slow, slow, quick, quick, slow.
    slow, quick, quick, slow, quick quick.

Repeat this, but ask the child to sing the appropriate words, for
example 'slow, slow, quick, quick, slow', on C as he plays.

Repeat this, asking the child to sing and move as you play.

Tune your voices.

Movement reinforces the meaning which is essential for
learning.

Step 9 Extending the memory

**If at first you *do* succeed, *don't* stop! A massive amount of
repetition over a long period is needed to learn anything
new. The more consolidated the learning of Middle C, the
easier future steps will become.**

The ability to use language requires several sorts of memory,
including the memory of pitched sounds and a considerable
memory span. Memory span can be increased while still
working on the pitched sound of C.

    Tune your voices.

    Ask the child to close his eyes while you play on the C tone bar the
    rhythm of a simple tune that he knows – for example, 'Baa, Baa,
    black sheep, Have you any wool?' Begin with only a short extract.
    Ask the child to open his eyes when you finish playing and copy
    the rhythm from memory.

    Repeat this activity, gradually increasing the length of rhythmic
    pattern played.

    Tune.

    Make up and play a short rhythmic pattern of just a few notes and
    encourage the child to respond with his own made-up rhythmic
    pattern, as if it were question and answer, for example:
    Question   *Answer*
    Slow, slow.   Quick, quick, slow.

    Reverse this, with the child questioning and you answering.

    Tune.

Ask the child to close his eyes and listen while you play short patterns of made-up sounds with a soft headed beater, for example:

Slow-quick-quick-slow-slow.
Slow-quick-slow-quick-slow.
Quick-quick-quick-quick-slow-slow.

After each pattern ask the child to open his eyes and, while you play it again, to sing the appropriate words while making the appropriate movements.

Tune.

Repeat the last activity, but this time, after he has moved and sung, ask him to sit down and play the pattern on the tone bar.

Tune.

Repeat the previous activity 'move and sing then play' with further patterns, but varying the beaters used. Take care to select the beaters when the child's eyes are closed.

Tune.

With the soft-headed beater and while the child's eyes are open, play four very loud, very slow sounds. Explain that you want him to jump with both feet together in time to the music.

Ask the child to repeat this, but to sing the word 'Jump' as he jumps and you play.

Tune.

Ask the child to close his eyes and listen carefully to find out how many times he must jump and sing. Play varying numbers of jumping sounds for him to jump and sing to with his eyes open.

Tune.

With a soft-headed beater, make up and play patterns to be acted, sung and played by the child, using the following movements:

Running steps for quick sounds
Walking steps for slow sounds
Jumping with both feet together for very slow sounds.

Tune.

A child needs a memory of basic movements before he can eventually perform or remember complex patterns of them. Handwriting involves complex patterns of many component movements.

Step 10   Developing co-ordination and control

Matching a movement to music requires maturity of motor control.

Control and co-ordination develop as a result of the massive repetition of experience which alone permits memory of the sensation. Handwriting calls for control and co-ordination through the brain of sight, hearing and precise movement; and to develop these you will need crayons, drawing paper and scissors as well as books of animal pictures and recordings of music that depicts animals – such as Prokoviev's *Peter and the Wolf* or *Carnival of the Animals* by Saint-Saëns.

Tune.

With the soft-headed beater, play the sounds of Step 9. Ask the child first to listen with closed eyes and then run, walk or jump with both feet to them, as appropriate.

Ask the child to think of animals that move in these ways. Search the picture books together for more ideas.

Listen to music on records and try out the jumping, walking and running to it.

Ask the child to draw, colour and cut out an animal for each movement for example:

Walking: Cow
Running: Mouse
Jumping: Rabbit, Kangaroo.

Tune.

Ask the child to watch you, and then with a hard-headed beater play on the tone bar at a suitable speed for hopping on one foot. Tell the child to hop one one foot in time to the sounds.

With the child still watching you, and with a soft-headed beater, play walking sounds at a similar speed to the hopping sounds, and remind the child to walk.

Tune.

Ask the child to close his eyes and listen, to decide whether to hop or to walk. Play with either the hard or soft headed beater until he has decided, when he must open his eyes and join in with the movement.

Tune.

Search the books again for animals that hop on one foot. If you cannot find any, use your imagination! Go through the records for suitable music and ask the child to hop to it.

Ask the child to draw, colour and cut out the real or pretend animal that hops on one foot. Add this picture to the collection.

Tune.

Search again for pictures of and music for an animal that crawls (e.g. a lion or cat). Ask the child to crawl to the music.

See if you can produce crawling sounds on the xylophone. Ask the child to help you choose the most effective beater. Ask the child to crawl to the sounds.

Add a crawling animal to your cut-out collection, and put them in a safe place for use later.

Tune.

Let the child practise all his animal movements to both xylophone and record music.

Movement itself will stimulate the chemical activity of the brain which is the basis of learning. The child who grasps the meaning of an activity quickly may be depriving himself of the massive repetition required for the development of control and kinaesthetic memory. Such children will not readily tolerate repetition unless the activities remain *interesting*. Muscle tone also requires regular activity if it is to be sufficiently well developed to aid control.

Step 11 Concentrating on tonal quality

Although sessions must remain short, they can (and probably will by now) be gradually increasing in length – possibly up to about twenty minutes, though this will vary according to the child's mood. Always finish while the session is still fun.

Just as the tonal quality of a flute is different from that of a violin or a piano, so the pitched sounds that make up speech vary in tonal quality according to which speech organs are being used to produce them. It is these speech sounds, codified by visual symbols, that are involved in reading. All the materials and aids used so far are needed to develop the child's learning of a wide variety of tonal qualities.

Tune.

Ask the child to close his eyes while you play the record of one of the pieces of 'animal music' you selected in step 10. Ask him to open his eyes and move to the music.

Repeat with all five pieces of walking, hopping, running, jumping and crawling music.

Tune.

Ask the child to listen to the extracts again, one at a time, and then try out all the beaters on the xylophone C to see which ones make the nearest sounds to each piece of music.

Tune.

With xylophone in hand and all the beaters, explore the house for C sounds which have similar tonal qualities to the various instruments which are used in the records to represent animals. Tape record these sounds and compare them to the original records.

Tune.

Remind the child to do his practice later on and discuss when would be the best time. Practice at this stage is still tuning the voice to C but can now include learning the individual sounds of the different beaters.

Follow-on Activities

1   Listen to *Peter and the Wolf* together, with eyes closed. Relax and enjoy the story. When you have done this several times, encourage the child to identify the animals in the extracts of the music, using the picture books and his own cut-out pictures, acting the movements and playing the movement sounds on the C tone bar.

2   Visit the children's library to search out animal picture and story books.

3   Visit a Zoo – take the tape recorder with you to collect more meaningful sounds – and let the child see, hear and smell the animals. Above all, have a lovely day – if the child enjoys the activity he will want to remember it.

4   Collect the vocabulary of the zoo. Encourage and help the child to start making a Picture Dictionary, for example:

Elephant: A large animal making loud sounds.

Ask the child to describe the elephant so that you can write a description in his book. Let the child see you transform his speech sounds into written words.

Step 12   The Animal Choir Practice

From now on, constantly repeat extracts from previous sessions and maintain activities like the Dinner Gong. Don't forget to praise and encourage the child.

Reading and spelling involve the learning of a symbol to represent every sound learnt.

The usual equipment, together with the collection of cut-out animals, some cardboard and any tape recorded sounds of animals you have managed to collect can now be used for further exploration of symbolic notation.

Tune.

Help the child to draw a fairly large one-rung ladder, colour it, stick it onto thick cardboard and cut it out.

Tune.

Remind the child how, when the bee sat on the one-rung picture ladder, the child tuned his voice to C. Find the bee, sit it on the rung of your new cardboard ladder and tune your voices.

Help the child to stick his cut-out animals from Step 10 onto cardboard and cut them out. You should both make the correct animal sound while you are working. If there is no cow, cat or mouse in the collection make them now. Other (or better) animals can be made during a wet afternoon.

Invite the child to choose an animal and sit it on the ladder in place of the bee. Ask him to pretend to be that animal and tune his voice before singing the correct animal sound on C.

Repeat this activity with as many different animals as possible. When some model animals have been made later, these can take their turn on the ladder.

Tune your own voices.

Suggest that the child arranges an animal choir practice and trains the animals while you accompany them on the xylophone. Draw a ladder for each animal. Suggest he begins by making sure all the animals are properly tuned in on C by tuning his voice for each animal in turn.

Suggest he rehearses each animal separately, first humming, then opening his mouth to make the correct animal sound

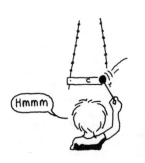

Ask the child to search his picture books for animals that make sounds like 'Maw' or 'Mo' or 'May' or 'Mar', if there are none in the choir already. Draw, colour and cut them out while making the correct animal sound.

The full choir sounds are now . . .

Hummmmmmmmmeeeeeeee   Hummmmmmmmmmoooooo   Hummmmmmmmmmmeow

Tape-record each animal rehearsing.

Add the pictures that go with all the animal sounds to the picture dictionary.

The act of vocalising aids the learning of the sound.

Follow-on Activities
1   Visit a farm. Search for story books about farms, and watch any television programme about farm life together with the child.

2   Make model animals from modelling clay, dough or papier mâché. Kneading of dough or clay helps to improve poor muscle tone in the hands, and the modelling activity will help develop hand/eye co-ordination. The models themselves can be used to help the understanding of pictorial representation of objects and their sounds.

3   Start making a model farm out of cardboard on a green cardboard field to house the model animals. Surround the field with a one-bar fence.

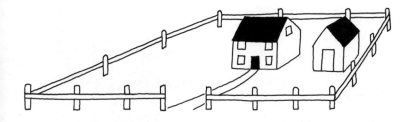

4   At storytime, read stories that include sound effects and have the child on your lap or nearby so that he can see you transform each written word into a sound. Point to the words as you read them.

5   Encourage the child to make up short stories with sound effects and to watch you while you transfer his speech sounds into written words and pictures.

Step 13 Long and short sounds

A child's hearing can vary daily. A regularly kept record book provides valuable information about these variations.

Speech sounds are made up of long and short pitched sounds. A recorder, simple home-made pipe or other blown instrument (such as a milk bottle blown across the top) can be used to ensure that the child hears and learns to recognise sounds of varying durations.

Tune.

Ask the child to help you tune your blown instrument(s) to the sound of the C tone bar by

1   Covering all the holes on the recorder.

2   Adjusting the level of water in a milk bottle until it produces 'C' when blown across the top.

3   Taking a cardboard cylinder (one with an internal diameter of about an inch and just over twelve inches long is a good starting point) and gradually reducing its length until it produces 'C'.

Tune.

Ask the child to watch while you demonstrate a short and then a long sound by blowing a short 'puff' and then a long 'puff'.

Tune.

Ask the child to play a short sound and then a very, very long sound.

Tune.

Ask the child to watch while you blow a very long sound, at the same time stretching up as tall as you can.

Tune.

Ask the child to lie down on the floor and, while you blow a long sound, to stretch out longer and longer, like a very long snake.

Tune.

Ask the child to curl up small, like a little snail while you play a very short sound.

Tune.

Reverse these activities with the child blowing the sounds while you act the snake and the snail.

Tune.

Ask the child to draw and cut out pictures of a snake and a snail to use on the picture ladder.

Tune.

Ask the child to play and then hum a short sound when he sees the snail on the ladder and a long sound when he sees the snake on the ladder.

Tune.

Ask the child to make up songs to act and sing on the sound of C, for example:
>   'I am a snake, wriggling along'
> or 'I'm a little snail all curled up small'

Tune.

Acting these movements helps to develop the child's spatial awareness. Moving to sounds will exercise the hearing system and help gain motor control; it will also exercise the eyes, since the muscles must move the eyes much more to help keep everything in focus as the body moves.

Seeing if the child can identify pictures representing aspects of sounds by making those sounds is a useful way of checking that a memory of the sound is beginning to develop.

Follow-on Activities
1   Make a model snail and snake for the farm, and also for use on the ladder. Using dough to make additional model animals, long after the farm is adequately equipped, will be a way to continue the development of hand/eye co-ordination; the animals can be baked and eated as a reward.
2   Make more blown instruments from cardboard cylinders, bamboo and plumbers' off-cuts.

Step 14 Organising practice time

Practice time is a useful means of revising the work done to date and assessing progress.

Practice now needs a little organising to ensure that the massive repetition of all activities, necessary for the eventual development of memory, is provided. Some of the activities will now require parental help, but the child should be encouraged to practise on his own whenever possible. The Practice or 'Test' card will eventually be used to test the child's progress, and should be added to at each step.

Tune.

Explain to the child that Cubs, Brownies, Scouts and Guides all have what is called a 'Test Card' to help them remember what they must practise – and so you are going to make a 'Test Card' for him.

Make up a small booklet out of thickish paper and draw up columns as shown below. There should be about thirty columns for 'Daily Practice' and enough pages eventually to cover about forty activities.

Date Started	Activity	Daily Practice														Test Passed
		1	2	3	4	5	6	7	8	9	10	11	12	....	30	

Tune.

Turn to Step 1 of this book. Quickly go through the contents demonstrating what was learnt. This can be summarised by 'playing up and down the ladder'. Write this down in the 'Activity' column of the card, and the date (today or tomorrow) on which practising starts.

Date Started	Activity	Daily Practice											Test Passed
		1	2	3	4	5	6	7	8	9	10	....	30	
	Playing up and down the ladder												

Turn to Step 2. Ask the child if he can tell you what he did for the first time in this second step. It was finding the first note, Middle C on the xylophone and then playing it. Add these to the card.

Turn to Step 3. Check what this adds and fill in the 'Activity' and 'Date Started' columns.

The Test Card will now read something like this:–

Date Started	Activity	Daily Practice										30	Test Passed
		1	2	3	4	5	6	7	8	9	....		
	Playing up and down the ladder												
	Reducing the xylophone to Middle C												
	Playing on Middle C												
	Tuning on Middle C												

Read through Step 4 to see if there is anything new to add to the test card. There is nothing from the session, but 'naming environmental sounds' can be added from the Follow-on activities.

Step 5 introduces loud and soft sounds and a variety of tone, using home made beaters. Add these three activities to the test card for practice.

Work through the book in this way until you reach this point (Step 14) again, by which time all the activities to be practised once a day will have been recorded on the 'Test Card'.

Each day the child practises an item for a few seconds he should tick it off in the Daily Practice column.

As each new step is covered, appropriate material should be added to the test card and included in the practice sessions. Don't forget to record the date on which practising starts.

Although many of the activities to be practised will now need some help from you, as accompanist and gramophone operator for example, don't hover over the child unnecessarily, as learning to organise his own practice time will teach him to work systematically and eventually develop self discipline.

Follow-on Activities
Make a 'Shaker' and a 'Jingle Bar' in readiness for Step 15.

Shaker

Half-fill with dried peas a small tin (or other container) that has a lid. Secure the lid firmly!

Jingle Bar

Find a cylindrical piece of wood about six inches long and between half and one inch in diameter. Attach two metal milk bottle tops to either end with nails or screws, allowing room for the tops to rattle about.

Step 15   Increasing spatial awareness

Children only achieve muscular control and co-ordination through much practice. Balance also has to be learnt.

Spatial awareness is needed to recognise the organised patterns of visual symbols codifying speech sounds. With the help of the xylophone, Shaker and Jingle Bar, the child can extend his understanding of his position in space while still practising the sound of C.

Make sure there is plenty of room, as you are going to ask the child to jump, run, walk, crawl and hop in all directions.

Tune.

Ask the child to spring up and down from a squatting position like a rabbit.

Tune.

Ask the child to spin round and round until he feels giddy.

Tune.

Ask the child to stand in the centre of the space, facing you, and let him hold a Shaker or Jingle Bar in the hand of his choice. Make sure he can learn by constant practice which is his left and which his right side. Give him something like a (toy) watch to wear proudly on his left wrist, to act as a reference point now and over the next few weeks.

Play very slow sounds for jumping and ask the child to jump to his left, singing the words 'Jump, jump, jump to the left' as he does so; remind him which is his left-hand side.

Repeat with 'Jump, jump, jump to the right'.

Tune.

Repeat with run, walk and crawl, reminding the child constantly which is his left and right side, and playing appropriate music on the xylophone.

Tune.

Repeat the activity with 'hopping' music – first on the left foot, singing:
    Hop, hop, hop ON my left
    Hop, hop, hop TO my LEFT
    Hop, hop, hop TO my RIGHT
Make sure that the child makes the appropriate movements.

Tune.

Repeat on the right foot:
    Hop, hop, hop ON my right
    Hop, hop, hop TO my RIGHT
    Hop, hop, hop TO my LEFT

Tune.

Ask the child to jump to the music again, but this time to jump forward, backward or round and round.

Tune.

Repeat with walk, run, crawl and hop.

Tune.

With the child, listen to a recording of a slow waltz and encourage him to roll head over heels in time to the music.

Tune.

Play the waltz rhythm on the xylophone and ask the child to roll head over heels in time to that.

Tune.

Ask the child to shake the Shaker or Jingle Bar in time to hopping, walking, running, crawling, jumping and rolling music on the xylophone. Let him use his preferred hand and encourage him to watch his hand as he plays and listens.

Tune.

Introduce changes in style of movement by asking the child to:
    bounce like a ball
    march like a tin soldier
    walk like a rubber man
    leap like a frog
    crawl like a cat
    slide like a snake
while you play appropriate music on the xylophone. You can help demonstrate this activity by reversing roles with the child, but do not always demonstrate before asking the child to perform the action – give him a chance to use his imagination.

Imagination is the product of previous experience. It is the linking of previous experiences in a hitherto unused way that leads to invention.

Follow-on Activity
Visit the local park or playground.

Ask the child to sit on a swing while you twist it round and round, then allow it to turn back.

Ask the child to spring up and down like a rabbit, then spin round and round until he feels giddy.

Ask the child to roll head over heels as many times as he can without stopping.

Early hearing problems can leave a child's balance mechanism unstimulated and thus in need of these kinds of activity.

Step 16   Stretching the imagination

Literacy is a marriage between the abilities to move, hear and see. Do not be tempted to omit any part of any session.

Activities exploring all parts of the body in various ways will develop the imagination, increase spatial and bodily awareness, and assist in co-ordination. The experiencing of tension in contrast to relaxation can be used to develop the ability to relax at will.

Tune.

Ask the child to play and hum in marching rhythm.

Tune.

Ask the child to act the part of a Tin Soldier while you play a marching rhythm on the xylophone.

Tune.

Ask the child to play and hum in a walking rhythm and then act the part of a Rubber Man walking, while you play.

Tune.

Explore recorded music that suggests the movements of a Tin Soldier and a Rubber Man, and move to them.

Tune.

Ask the child to act a Rubber Soldier to marching rhythm on the xylophone, and then a Tin Man to walking rhythm.

Tune.

Ask the child to lie on the floor and make each part of his body in turn stiff like the Tin Soldier, for example:–

toes, ankles, knees, legs, hips, waist, wrists,
elbows, arms, shoulders, neck.

Tune.

Ask the child to make each part of his body in turn 'floppy' like the Rubber Man.

Tune.

Play short patterns of quick and slow sounds on the xylophone and ask the child (still on the floor) to move each part of his body in turn in time to the music. Tell him to watch as he moves.

Tune.

A person who has never experienced the sensation of relaxation will not understand what is meant by the term.

Follow-on Activities

1 Add all the parts of the body to the picture dictionary.

2 Encourage the child to make up a story about the Tin Soldier and his friend the Rubber Man for him to act and you to write down.

3 While you are out walking with the child, stand on the pavement and watch and listen to the cars as they come and go. (Preparation for Step 17.)

4 Take the child to a railway station. Watch and listen for the trains coming in from a distance, entering the station and going off again into the distance. Sing the train sounds 'clickerty-clack, clickerty-clack, clickerty-clack'. Make a good tape recording of all these sounds to use in the next step (17).

Step 17   The Train Game

The ability to recognise very small changes in loudness levels and duration patterns develops as the result of much practice.

The Train Game will teach the child to recognise some of the very small changes involved in language. Tracking of the sound source with the eyes will also develop the learning of distance, direction and speed of movement, and aid development of the eye muscles.

Tune.

When you hear a car approaching from a distance, ask the child to come to the window and watch and listen to the car come and go.

Tune.

Explain to the child that you are going to play sounds representing a car coming and going. Explaining what is happening as you demonstrate, play a series of notes very softly, gradually getting louder and louder until the 'car' has passed, and then softer and softer as it goes off into the distance.

Tune.

Ask the child to copy the sounds of the car coming and going.

Tune.

Ask the child to pretend that the table or a chair is a tunnel and to take a toy car through it, singing softly while the car is in the tunnel and getting gradually louder as it comes out again. Accompany him on the xylophone.

Tune.

Ask the child to make a paper tunnel for the car to travel through and repeat the previous activity.

Tune.

Play the recordings of train sounds you made at the railway station and match the sounds on the xylophone singing 'clickerty-clack' at the same time. Ask the child to move round the room in time to the music.

Tune.

Ask the child to copy the sounds on the xylophone.

Tune.

Help the child to draw a picture of a train coming in from a distance. Make sure it is moving from left to right.

Explain that when this picture sits on the ladder the sound should start very softly and gradually get louder and louder.

Tune.

Help the child to draw a picture of a train going off into the distance, still moving from left to right.

Explain that when this picture sits on the ladder the sound should begin loudly and gradually get softer and softer.

Tune.

Place the pictures on the ladder and ask the child to play and sing the appropriate sounds.

Tune.

The visual tracking of moving sound sources develops the learning of distance, direction and speed of movement, and aids the development of the eye muscles. It is important that a train approaching should produce a drawing that is shaped ◄▦▦▦ , and going off into the distance a drawing shaped ▦▦▦► , as this ties in with symbols that will be introduced in a later step.

Follow-on Activities

1   Add the Train Game to the test card for practice.

2   Make a model Railway station and model train to stand near the Farm. You can gradually build up a model village to add to the collection of support material for playtime, in which further games can be improvised.

3   Explore your 'odds and ends' for objects that make the sound of C and compose and record a 'Junk Symphony'.

Step 18   Hunt the Toffee

Although much repetition is necessary for the learning of every sound it must always be made interesting and fun.

Like the Train Game, Hunt the Toffee encourages the child to listen to the small changes in loudness levels which are so very important for language development, while providing more repetition of the note C. As a game it is both interesting and rewarding for the child as the finder eats the toffee!

Tune.

Tell the child that a toffee which is hidden in the room can be found by listening to the sound of the xylophone being played. Demonstrate by walking with the child and playing the xylophone increasingly louder as you approach a visible toffee and increasingly softer as you move away from it.

Tune.

Have a practice run with the child moving to and from a visible toffee while you play on the xylophone to match his movements.

Tune.

Ask the child to close his eyes or leave the room while you hide the toffee. When the search begins play louder as he moves nearer and softer as he moves futher away from the hidden toffee. When he finds the toffee, let him eat it.

Tune.

Repeat the activity trying to make the search last longer by hiding the toffee in a more difficult place. Don't try to economise on toffees – if the child finds it he must have it, even it it must be eaten later on.

Tune.

Record in the record book how, if at all, the child appears to hear small changes of loudness. This gives important information about his hearing.

Step 19 Introducing the piano

The sound quality that is heard is the one learnt.

Since a piano usually produces a better quality of sound than a xylophone, if there is one available, it is worthwhile including it as early as possible in the activities. If you do not have one yourself, perhaps a friend, local nursery school or even a friendly music shop will allow access.

Later on in this session, the piano and xylophone will be played together. Most modern pianos and good quality xylophones will be tuned to concert pitch. Some older pianos will be pitched considerably lower (though they can be brought up to concert pitch by a piano tuner over a period of time), and some poor quality xylophones may be pitched quite differently. Before using the piano, check that its notes from middle C upwards are as nearly as possible the same as those of the xylophone you have been using.

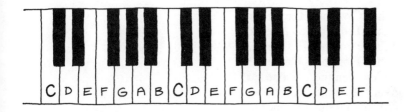

Tune your voices.

Ask the child to look at the piano keyboard while you point out that there are black and white keys that make a musical sound when pushed gently down.

Ask the child to play some of the sounds first on the black keys and then on the white ones.

Point out that the black keys are in patterns of twos and threes.

Ask the child to play all the patterns of two black notes counting 'one, two' as he plays.

Ask the child to play all the groups of three black notes counting 'one, two, three' as he plays.

Tune.

Explain to the child what is meant by the middle of anything.

Play a game round the house with the child touching the middle of everything he can find. Ask him to touch his own middle (waist).

Tune.

Explain to the child that he can make the same sound as that of the tone bar – C – on the piano. Show him that there are many Cs on the piano by pointing to the white note which is to the left of each group of two black notes (when facing the piano).

Ask the child to play all the Cs he can find on the piano.

Ask him to find the C which seems to him to be nearest the middle of the piano (there is often a lock there). This C in the middle of the piano is the Middle C to which you have been tuning your voices since the very first step.

Ask the child to play middle C on the piano while you play on the xylophone, and to tune his voice to the sound.

Suggest that the child finds all the Cs on the piano whenever he is near one, and plays and tunes his voice to middle C.

Ask the child to put all the tone bars back on the xylophone and then take the xylophone to the piano. Help him to play

C on the piano	and then C on the	C tone bar
D on the piano	and then D on the	D tone bar
E on the piano	and then E on the	E tone bar
F on the piano	and then F on the	F tone bar
G on the piano	and then G on the	G tone bar
A on the piano	and then A on the	A tone bar
B on the piano	and then B on the	B tone bar
C on the piano	and then C on the	C tone bar

and so on until the xylophone is complete. Explain that later on when he has learnt all the notes of the xylophone the piano will provide some extra ones.

Explain that when playing 'up' the piano one must move to the right, which, as he has just found out, is the same as playing up the xylophone or musical ladder.

Tune.

Ask Dad or an Uncle to help by singing the sound of C in his lower voice, while you sing in your middle voice. Explain to the child that the different Cs on the piano are just different members of the C family.

The matching of the sounds of the xylophone and piano will encourage accurate listening for the best quality of sound.

Follow-on Activity
Draw and colour a piano keyboard.

Step 20   Feeling and counting the beat

Regulated movement is the basis of life and growth – this is rhythm. Rhythmic movement of sounds is the basis of language.

The xylophone and a collection of recordings of marches and waltzes can be used to continue developing the feeling of the musical beat that is started in the womb when the child feels and hears his mother's heartbeat. Counting and moving in time to music is a useful way of acquiring eye/foot co-ordination.

Tune.

Explain to the child that you will be playing walking sounds on the xylophone, and when you play
    One sound he must walk one step
    two sounds he must walk two steps
    three sounds he must walk three steps
    four sounds he must walk four steps.
Demonstrate, playing the xylophone as you walk while the child watches and listens.

Ask the child to walk the correct number of steps *after* listening to what you play. Accompany him as he walks.

Ask the child to emphasise the count 'One' in each group of steps he walks and counts

ONE two
or ONE two three
or ONE two three four

Tune.

Find recordings of simple waltzes for counting up to three, or marches for counting up to two or four. Let the child move in time to the music counting 'one two, one two, one two . . .' or 'one two three, one two three, one two three . . .' and so on.

Tune.

Ask the child to draw the steps his feet take when he moves to each group of 1,2,3 or 4 sounds. Ask him to move and count to each group in turn before drawing it.

Counting One   👣
Counting to two   👣 👣
Counting to three 👣 👣 👣
Counting to four 👣 👣 👣 👣

Tune.

Explain to the child that it might be quicker to draw little black circles instead of footsteps, that is ● instead of 👣

Repeat the previous activity, drawing ● instead of 👣

    Count one   ●
    Count to two   ●●
    Count to three ●●●
    Count to four   ●●●●

Tune.

Play random patterns of 2,3, or 4 sounds on the xylophone for the child to draw.

Counting and moving in time to music is a useful step forward in the acquiring of eye/foot co-ordination and spatial awareness. Using visual symbols to represent groups of sounds develops the ability to recognise the spatially-organised patterns of visual symbols involved in literacy skills.

Step 21   Skipping to music

Handwriting skills require a developed kinaesthetic memory (memory of sensation) of the component movements.

Skipping requires the memory of a complex mixture of basic movements in the same way that speech requires the memory of the complex mixture of musical ingredients. The memory of each of the basic movements must be developed in a logical, step-by-step way.

Recordings of as many different dances as possible with a skipping rhythm are used to extend the child's co-ordination and control and develop the kinaesthetic memory of the movement.

Listen to the quietest sounds you can hear.

Tune.

Preferably working in an uncarpeted area, ask the child to close his eyes and listen while you walk across the floor first on tiptoe and then normally. Ask him if he heard any difference in the sound.

Repeat this asking the child to watch what you were doing.

Tune.

Ask the child to copy you walking, first on tip toe and then normally.

Tune.

Ask the child to close his eyes and listen carefully to you walking across the room again, first normally, then on tiptoe and finally changing from one to the other. Ask the child to tell you when you change and what you are doing just by listening to the sounds made.

Tune.

Make up patterns of normal and tiptoe walking for the child to listen to with his eyes closed and then copy from memory with his eyes open.

Tune.

Ask the child to hop alternately one step on his left foot, one step on his right foot, slowly across the room while you play slow sounds on the xylophone.

Ask the child to keep in time with the xylophone as you gradually quicken your playing to skipping speed.

Ask the child to close his eyes and listen to you 'skipping'. Ask him to open his eyes and try to copy your movement while you play the xylophone.

Tune.

Ask the child to hop slowly on alternate feet across the floor again. Make sure he is putting his heel down, and draw his attention to the fact.

Tune.

Ask the child to hop slowly across the room on alternate feet on tiptoe.

Tune.

Ask the child to hop slowly twice on each foot, alternating feet every two steps.

Tune.

Ask the child to hop slowly twice on each foot again but this time the first hop on each foot should be with the heel down, the second hop on the toes. Accompany him on the xylophone as he hops.

Tune.

Play recordings of skipping music for the child to skip round the room, matching his movement to the music.

Tune.

It may take several sessions on these activities before the child begins to skip. Once he is doing so, make sure you revise the movement every day as it takes a long time to establish.

Step 22   Musical Parcel and Musical Snap

The young child's brain is very plastic. Without constant revision to establish learning permanently, information will gradually be forgotten.

Both 'Musical Parcel' and 'Musical Snap' are attractive ways of revising previous activities and useful ways of confirming where any difficulties lie. The possibility of reward will encourage the child to perform as well as he can.

Cards about the size of half a postcard, crayons, brown paper, string and a small box of favourite small sweets will be needed, as well as the usual equipment.

Tune.

On each card help the child to draw and colour a picture of each sound-making activity that has been carried out in steps 1-22. Check with the practice test card that all the activities have been covered.

Tune.

Musical Parcel
Wrap the small box of sweets and tie it with string as if in a parcel.

Place a card on the parcel, wrap another sheet of paper around it and tie up with another piece of string.

Continue like this until you have used up all the picture cards and have a large parcel.

Tune.

Ask the child to lie flat on the floor and hold the parcel between his feet.

Explain that when you play on the xylophone he must bring his feet up holding the parcel until he can take it in his hands.

Still holding the parcel in his hands, he must stretch out tall, arms above his head, before bringing his arms back again to give the parcel back to his feet.

If the parcel is in his hands when you stop playing, he must take off a layer of paper and make the sound pictured on the card. If he cannot he forfeits a point. He also forfeits a point if he drops the parcel. When he reaches the sweets he must give you one for every point forfeited, but can keep the rest.

Note in the Record book every picture he has difficulty with. Later see if a little extra practice will help, or whether it appears to be a problem with which he cannot cope.

Musical Snap

Divide a small box of sweets between you as 'counters'.

Using the card pictures as playing cards, place them face down in front of the child.

Explain that while you are playing the xylophone he is to pick up each card in turn, look at it and then put it down, face up, to the side of the pile. Each time you stop playing, he must immediately make the correct sound of the picture he is holding in tune to the C tone bar, *before* you start playing again. (Allow him about four seconds by counting silently to four.)

Tell him you will pay him a 'counter' each time he succeeds in making the right sound in time, but he must pay you one if he does not.

Once again, record any difficulties in the record book.

Rewards and encouragement must be easily recognised at this stage, but neither reward too easily nor too rarely: use your common sense.

Step 23   The first Test

Now you have worked through all the steps of Stage One, the Test Card can be used as a basis for testing the memory of each of the auditory components that exists. This is necessary before moving on to the second stage.

Your test card could now be looking something like the card overleaf.

Date	Activity	Daily Practice (about 30 spaces)															Test Passed
		1	2	3	4	5	6	7	8	9		26	27	28	29	30	
Monday May 5th	Playing up and down the ladder	✓	✓	✓	✓	✓	✓	✓	✓	✓	✓	✓	✓	✓	✓	✓	
,,	Reducing the xylophone to middle 'C'	✓	✓	✓	✓	✓	✓	✓	✓	✓	✓	✓	✓	✓	✓	✓	
,,	Playing middle 'C'	✓	✓	✓	✓	✓	✓	✓	✓	✓	✓	✓	✓	✓	✓	✓	
,,	Tuning to middle 'C'	✓	✓	✓	✓	✓	✓	✓	✓	✓	✓	✓	✓	✓	✓	✓	
,,	Loud sounds of 'C'	✓	✓	✓	✓	✓	✓	✓	✓	✓	✓	✓	✓	✓	✓	✓	
,,	Soft sounds of 'C'	✓	✓	✓	✓	✓	✓	✓	✓	✓	✓	✓	✓	✓	✓	✓	
,,	Sounds with different beaters on 'C'	✓	✓	✓	✓	✓	✓	✓	✓	✓	✓	✓	✓	✓	✓	✓	
,,	Naming sounds of the environment	✓	✓	✓	✓	✓	✓	✓	✓	✓	✓	✓	✓	✓	✓	✓	
,,	Bright sounds	✓	✓	✓	✓	✓	✓	✓	✓	✓	✓	✓	✓	✓	✓	✓	
,,	Dull sounds	✓	✓	✓	✓	✓	✓	✓	✓	✓	✓	✓	✓	✓	✓	✓	
,,	Fast moving sounds	✓	✓	✓	✓	✓	✓	✓	✓	✓	✓	✓	✓	✓	✓	✓	
,,	Slow moving sounds	✓	✓	✓	✓	✓	✓	✓	✓	✓	✓	✓	✓	✓	✓	✓	
,,	Listen to extracts from 'Peter and the Wolf' (story time)	✓	✓	✓	✓	✓	✓	✓	✓	✓	✓	✓	✓	✓	✓	✓	Characters identified DATE
,,	Practice tuning voice and singing MOO	✓	✓	✓	✓	✓	✓	✓	✓	✓	✓	✓	✓	✓	✓	✓	
,,	MEE	✓	✓	✓	✓	✓	✓	✓	✓	✓	✓	✓	✓	✓	✓	✓	
,,	MEOW	✓	✓	✓	✓	✓	✓	✓	✓	✓	✓	✓	✓	✓	✓	✓	
,,	MAW	✓	✓	✓	✓	✓	✓	✓	✓	✓	✓	✓	✓	✓	✓	✓	
,,	MO	✓	✓	✓	✓	✓	✓	✓	✓	✓	✓	✓	✓	✓	✓	✓	
,,	MAY	✓	✓	✓	✓	✓	✓	✓	✓	✓	✓	✓	✓	✓	✓	✓	
,,	MAR	✓	✓	✓	✓	✓	✓	✓	✓	✓	✓	✓	✓	✓	✓	✓	

How to use the Test Card

Tell the child that you are going to test him to see how well he has learnt what he has been practising, and that when he passes the whole test he will have a badge to wear.

Ask the child to perform each activity on the Test Card in turn and if he does so accurately, write the date in the 'Test Passed' column. If he does not manage to pass all the tests (and this is quite common at this stage) leave the appropriate space blank.

When the child has had more practice on the test activities not previously passed, test him again – but make sure at least a week has passed between practising and testing, to be certain that any successfully-performed activity has been properly learnt.

Date	Activity	Daily Practice (about 30 spaces)									…						Test Passed
		1	2	3	4	5	6	7	8	9		26	27	28	29	30	
May 5th	Long sounds	✓	✓	✓	✓	✓	✓	✓	✓	✓	✓ ✓	✓	✓	✓	✓	✓	
,,	Short sounds	✓	✓	✓	✓	✓	✓	✓	✓	✓	✓ ✓	✓	✓	✓	✓	✓	
Thursday May 8	Jumping sounds and actions	✓	✓	✓	✓	✓	✓	✓	✓	✓	✓ ✓	✓	✓	✓	✓	✓	
,,	Walking sounds and actions	✓	✓	✓	✓	✓	✓	✓	✓	✓	✓ ✓	✓	✓	✓	✓	✓	
,,	Running sounds and actions	✓	✓	✓	✓	✓	✓	✓	✓	✓	✓ ✓	✓	✓	✓	✓	✓	
,,	Hopping sounds and actions	✓	✓	✓	✓	✓	✓	✓	✓	✓	✓ ✓	✓	✓	✓	✓	✓	
,,	Crawling sounds and actions	✓	✓	✓	✓	✓	✓	✓	✓	✓	✓ ✓	✓	✓	✓	✓	✓	
Sunday May 11	Tin Soldier actions of all parts of the body	✓	✓	✓	✓	✓	✓	✓	✓	✓	✓ ✓	✓	✓	✓			
,,	Rubber Man actions of all parts of the body	✓	✓	✓	✓	✓	✓	✓	✓	✓	✓ ✓	✓	✓				
Fri. 16	The Train sounds	✓	✓	✓	✓	✓	✓	✓	✓	✓	✓						
Thurs. 22	'C' on the piano	✓	✓	✓	✓	✓	✓	✓	✓	✓	✓						
,,	Play each Tone Bar and the piano note	✓	✓	✓	✓	✓	✓	✓	✓	✓	✓						
Monday May 26	Play and walk one step; stressing the step	✓	✓	✓	✓	✓	✓	✓	✓	✓	✓						
,,	Play and walk two steps; stressing the first step	✓	✓	✓	✓	✓	✓	✓	✓	✓	✓						
,,	Play and walk three steps; stressing the first step	✓	✓	✓	✓	✓	✓	✓	✓	✓	✓						
,,	Play and walk four steps; stressing the first step	✓	✓	✓	✓	✓	✓	✓	✓	✓	✓						
Friday June 6	Hop on left foot and then on right foot	✓	✓	✓													
,,	Skipping movement and playing on xylophone	✓	✓	✓													

If he still has difficulties with some tests, and the record book and possibly the test card show that he has consistently had such a problem, seek medical advice.

When the child has successfully passed all the tests, award him the Stage One proficiency badge and move on to Stage Two.

Proficiency Badge
Using fairly stiff white cardboard, cut out a circular section of approximately one inch diameter. On this draw a picture of a 'Bee'. Colour the Bee in the usual colours of black and yellow. On the back of the badge attach a safety pin by means of sellotape. The words 'Stage One' should be printed on the badge as shown in the sketch.

The 'Bee' is chosen to represent the pre-notation stage.

STAGE TWO

Step 24   The story of Mr and Mrs Humpty

This story will help prepare your child for stage two.

> Humpty Dumpty sat on a wall,
> Humpty Dumpty had a great fall.
> All the King's horses and all the King's men
> Couldn't put Humpty together again.

Once upon a time there was a village surrounded by a wall. The folk who lived there were called Dumptys and they all looked just like eggs, some brown, some white. Not only did they look just like eggs, but they were all roly-poly like eggs, too. As long as they were walking or running along the ground they had no trouble at all keeping their balance, so most of them stayed there to be safe; but occasionally the more adventurous villagers, wanting to see what was over the wall, climbed up on to it – and nearly always fell off. Sometimes they hurt themselves so badly that even the King's men couldn't put them together again.

One day a certain Mr Humpty, who looked just like a dark brown egg, was watching a cat walking along a particularly narrow wall, holding its tail up as if it was helping it to balance. That gave Mr Humpty an idea. 'If I grew a tail,' he thought, perhaps it would help me balance on the wall.' So he did, and it worked so well that soon all the villagers had grown tails.

One day, Mr Humpty was sitting on the wall admiring the view when along came a white lady Dumpty. She climbed, with some difficulty, onto the wall and sat next to Mr Humpty and they talked and talked. They enjoyed each other's company so much that they met again and again. Realising that they were in love with each other, they decided to get married. They often used to sit on the wall together, and Mr Humpty made Mrs Humpty a little ladder to make it easier for her to climb up and down.

After a while, Mrs Humpty had a baby – who looked just like Mr Humpty. Sometimes she used to take baby Humpty with her when she went to sit on the wall and, as he was much too small to climb up for himself, she carried him on her back, just like African mothers do.

Grandma Humpty was very eager to see the new baby, so she came to visit the family. Mr and Mrs Humpty wanted her to come and sit on the wall to admire the view, but were a little worried that she might fall off as she was rather too old to grow a tail. But Grandma was a large, cuddly lady, and they found she could balance on the wall quite easily, even without a tail.

The whole Humpty family spent so much time sitting on the wall that they got very good at balancing and their tails grew straight and strong.

One day they decided it would be great fun if they all learnt to sing – and we will be finding out just how they did it quite soon!

Step 25 Mr and Mrs Humpty start to sing

A sound notated is well on the way to being remembered.

Modelling material will be needed to make Mr and Mrs
Humpty, who will be used to introduce traditional notation.

Help the child to make two egg-shaped Humpty Dumptys out of
plasticine, modelling clay, papier mâché or dough. One should be
black or brown and the other white.

Ask the child which egg looks most like Mr Humpty in the
story and which most like Mrs Humpty.

Tune.

Remind the child how, in step 20, he counted in time to music.
Ask him to count as you play groups of two or three notes on the
xylophone.

Tune.

Tell the child that you can use humming to count wih the voice.
Demonistrate by counting 'one, two' then humming 'mmm,
mmm'. Ask the child to copy you.

Tune.

Ask the child to pick up the egg that looks like Mr Humpy (the
brown or black one) and explain that when Mr Humpty tunes his
voice he makes the sound 'mmm' for just one count for each
sound on the xylophone. Ask him to tune his voice like Mr
Humpty.

Tune.

Ask the child to pick up the egg that looks like Mrs Humpty (the
white one) and explain that she makes a sound twice as long as Mr
Humpty, so when she tunes her voice she makes the sound
'mmm-mmm' for two counts for each sound on the xylophone.
Ask him to tune his voice like Mrs Humpty, playing only one
sound on the xylophone, even though it will probably fade away
before the two counts.

Tune.

Ask the child to pick up Mr Humpty when you hum for one
count, or Mrs Humpty when you hum for two.

Tune.

You pick up the Humptys one at a time and ask the child to hum
the right number of counts according to which one you show him.
Remember, only one stroke on the xylophone.

Tune.

While moving towards notation, the work with Mr and Mrs
Humpty provides still more repetition of the note C.

Step 26   A new name – 'Doh'

We have about forty pitched sounds to learn in speech – which must eventually be blended together.

As soon as you start dealing with more than one of anything the use of names becomes necessary, and you will soon be moving on to more notes.

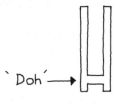

Tune.

Ask the child to draw a large one-rung ladder. Help him to stick it onto cardboard and cut it out. Explain that the rung of the ladder has a name, just as he does, and its name is 'Doh'.

Tune.

Take the child to the stairs, steps or ladder and explain that this time, when he climbs onto the first step or rung he must be polite and, after first tuning his voice, sing on the same sound 'Good morning Doh'. Accompany him on the xylophone.

Tune.

Tell the child that when Mr and Mrs Humpty sit on the ladder, they not only sing their own sound, but also the name of the ladder-rung, so Mr Humpty sings 'mmm, doh' and Mrs Humpty sings 'mmm-mmm, doh-oh'.

Ask the child to put Mr Humpty on the ladder, to tune his own voice and then sing Mr Humpty's sounds:
    Tune, mmm, Doh.

Repeat this with Mrs Humpty:
    Tune, mmm-mmm, Doh-oh.

Tune.

Vary this activity by you placing Mr or Mrs Humpty on the ladder and the child playing the sound softly, tuning his own voice and then singing Mr or Mrs Humpty's sounds as appropriate. Remember, only one stroke on the xylophone each time.

Tune.

Don't forget to continue with the practice/test card and the record book.

Step 27 Sound and silence

Sounds and silences are related. The louder the so-called silence, the noisier sound must become before we recognise the difference.

A study of silence helps reverse some of the damage being done by constant loud noisy background, which can cause poor speech discrimination. It also improves the child's threshold of listening.

Tune.

Ask the child to find his one-step ladder. Explain that sometimes the rung of the ladder gets very tired of people climbing all over him so he has had a sign made to show everyone when he wants a rest. The sign looks like this: ▬

Tune.

Explain that when the sign hangs on the ladder everyone must creep away quietly, without making any sound at all so the step called 'Doh' can have a rest.

Tune.

Let the child practise putting his fingers to his lips and creeping away quietly whenever he sees the rest sign on the ladder.

Tune.

Ask the child to make his own rest sign. When you hold up your rest sign, get him to pick his up, put his fingers to his lips and become absolutely silent.

Tune.

Sound and silence is relative, therefore silence should be as silent as possible!

Follow-on Activities
1   Introduce the rest sign to the family or class as a signal for silence – but resist the temptation to overuse it!

2   Re-read 'The Story of Mr and Mrs Humpty' to the child.

Step 28   Some more members of the Humpty family

Speech sounds vary in duration.

The Humpty family is used to symbolise different durations of sounds. They gradually become a very useful way of collecting information about the child's hearing.

Tune.

Remind the child of the story you read him about the Humptys, and how they grew tails.

Help the child to make another Mr and Mrs Humpty, complete with tails, out of modelling material.

Tune.

Ask the child to sit Mr Humpty on the Doh rung of the ladder, tune his voice and then sing both Mr Humpty's sounds:
    Tune – mmm – Doh.

Repeat with Mrs Humpty:
    Tune – mmm-mmm – Doh-oh.

Tune.

Help the child to make a Mrs Humpty carrying a baby on her back. The baby is a little boy and black or brown coloured like his father.

Tune.

Explain that when Mrs Humpty has the baby on her back she must sing an even longer sound, her own 'mmm-mmm' plus an extra 'mmm' for the baby. With the baby on her back, her sound is now 'mmm-mmm-mmm' for three counts.
    When she climbs onto the 'Doh' rung of the ladder with baby Humpty on her back she must sing 'Doh-oh-oh' as well.

Ask the child to sit Mrs Humpty and baby on the ladder, tune and sing both their sounds:
    Tune, mmm-mmm-mmm, Doh-oh-oh.
Remember, however long the note, play only one stroke on the xylophone.

Tune.

Tell the child that you will sing the sound of Mr Humpty or Mrs Humpty or Mrs Humpty with baby on her back, and he must then pick up the right member of the family.

Tune.

Reverse this – you pick up the Humptys and ask the child to sing the appropriate sound.

Tune.

Help the child to make a granny Humpty. Granny looks like a fat Mrs Humpty, but has no tail as she was too old to grow one.

Granny Humpty's sound is four times as long as Mr Humpty's or twice as long as Mrs Humpty's so is made to the count of four:
'mmm – mmm – mmm – mmm'.

When Granny Humpty sits on the ladder she sings
'Doh-oh-oh-oh' as well.

Ask the child to sit Granny Humpty on the ladder, tune and sing both her sounds,
Tune, mmm-mmm-mmm-mmm, Doh-oh-oh-oh.

Tune.

Ask the child to draw pictures of the whole Humpty family.

Stick them onto cardboard and cut them out. You will be using them over and over again.

Tune.

Place the members of the Humpty family you have drawn and cut out on the rung of the ladder in random order and ask the child to sing the appropriate sound for that Humpty sitting on the ladder. Accompany each sound with only one stroke on the xylophone, even though it will not last to the end of every sound.

Tune.

Recognising the duration of a sound requires very careful listening.

Step 29　A new note – G

Sounds are learnt one at a time after much repetition. The work on C must be kept up while learning the new note, or the child will begin to forget it.

The G above Middle C appears to be the second note that children most easily learn.

With all the tone bars on the xylophone and a soft-headed beater, ask the child to play the C tone bar and hum its sound.
　Remind the child that the tone bar has its name C engraved on it.

Tune on C.

Ask the child to play the next tone bar with D engraved on it and hum its sound before lifting it off the xylophone with both hands.

Tune on C.

Ask the child to play the third tone bar with E engraved on it and hum its sound before lifting it off with both hands.

Tune on C.

Repeat with the fourth tone bar engraved F.

Tune on C.

Ask the child to play the fifth tone bar with G engraved on it and hum its sound. This is the note that is now to be learnt. Remove all the remaining tone bars, leaving only C and G on the xylophone.

Tune on C and then to G.

Explain to the child that 'Tuning' now means playing first C and humming to it and then G and humming to that.

Tune your voices to C and G.

Ask the child to draw a ladder with two rungs, one at the bottom and one half way up to look like the xylophone.

Ask the child to play the musical step G softly each time you point to the second rung of the ladder.

Tune to C and G.

Reverse this – you play when the child points.

Tune to C and G.

Remind the child how he touched his toes to C.
　Liken the note G which is halfway up the musical ladder to the part of the body halfway up – the waist or middle.

Tune to C and G.

Ask the child to touch his middle when you play the G tone bar softly.

Tune to C and G.

Carry the xylophone round the house to find objects that make the G sound when tapped, blown, moved or shaken.

Tune to C and G.

The young child's brain is growing very rapidly, which is why work must be constantly reinforced to ensure that it does not outgrow the learning.

The constant tuning to C and G is one way of preventing the child from forgetting C. It demonstrates the way old activities should be continually reinforced by revision, while spending the greatest time (about twice as much) on the new material: a sort of *learning sandwich.*

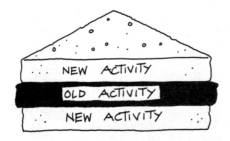

Step 30 Extending pitch discrimination

The child must learn to distinguish between and recognise, via visual symbols, approximately forty different pitched chords, with the greatest variety of tonal quality, duration-patterns and intensity-levels, if he is to read fluently.

Now that a second note has been introduced, pitch discrimination can be extended. The greater the distance between two pitched sounds the easier it is to discriminate between them – another reason why the G above Middle C is learnt next. It is usually the upper extreme of the young child's 'controlled' vocal range.

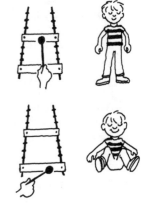

   This work will eventually provide important information about the child's hearing, so do not forget to keep the record book up to date.

   Tune to C and G.

   Turn to Step 5 (page 17) and repeat all the work on loud and soft sounds but on the note G instead of middle C.

   Tune (C & G).

   Ask the child to play the sound G on the xylophone, then take it round the house with him searching out more sounds of G.

   Tune (C & G).

   Play G on the xylophone and explain that when he hears G he must stand up, but when he hears C he must sit down, but that he must listen with his eyes closed.

   Play Cs and Gs in random order for the child to sit down or stand up.

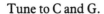

   Tune (C & G).

   Repeat, but this time ask the child to touch his toes for C and his middle for G.

   Tune (C & G).

Practice now means repeating all the activities on the test card, which should be added to at every session.

   Each step now contains more material, so may be lasting as long as twenty minutes, which is fine as long as it is fun. Don't forget that some steps may take several days.

Step 31 Some useful signs

The written word is made up entirely of sounds codified by visual symbols.

Now the child understands the meaning of *loud* and *soft*, their symbolic representation can be introduced.

Tune (C and G throughout this step).

Ask the child to place on the ladder an animal that makes very loud sounds, a cow for example. Explain that there is a 'magic' sign that can now be used for very loud sounds which is much easier to draw than an animal and is 'ff'. Help him to draw the sign on a card.

Tune.

Ask the child to place on the ladder an animal that makes very soft sounds, a mouse for example. Explain that the 'magic' sign for very soft sounds is 'pp'. Draw the sign on a card.

Tune.

Find an animal which makes fairly loud sounds, e.g. a dog, and explain that the sign for loud sounds is 'f'. Draw the sign on a card.

Tune.

Find an animal that makes fairly soft sounds, e.g. a cat, and explain that the sign for soft sounds is 'p'. Draw the sign on a card.

Tune.

Play samples of 'ff ', 'pp', 'f ' and 'p' sounds in random order on the G tone bar, ask the child to copy the sound and select the sign that goes with it.

Tune.

Show the child the sign cards in random order and ask him to play the correct sound, first on G then on C.

Tune.

Place the sign cards on the ladder one by one on either rung and ask the child to play the correct sound on the correct tone bar.

Tune.

Show the child the picture of a train coming in from the distance (from Step 17), and ask him to play the sound on the G tone bar.

Repeat this with the picture of a train going away into the distance.

Tune.

Explain that these pictures can be replaced by easily drawn signs

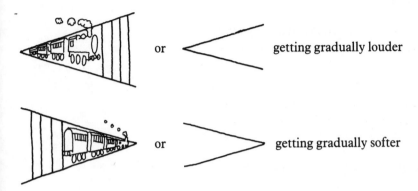

or   getting gradually louder

or   getting gradually softer

Show these signs to the child in random order and ask him to play the appropriate sounds on the G tone bar.

Tune.

Place the signs on either rung of the ladder, one by one, and ask the child to play the correct sound on the correct tone bar.

Tune.

Twice as much work should be carried out on the new sound G as on the old sound C. The learning sandwich (Step 29) explains why.

Step 32   Drawing Rhythmograms

The co-ordination of hearing, vision and movement is required for all literacy skills.

Drawing rhythmograms to symbolise each quality of sound as it is heard develops the three-way co-ordination required for literacy skills.

Tune (C & G).

Think of simple melodies and play their rhythm only on the G tone bar.
    Explain to the child that you want him to draw the sound by using.

short lines for short sounds	‖‖‖
long lines for loud sounds	‖‖‖‖
thick lines for loud sounds	‖‖‖‖
thin lines for soft sounds	‖‖‖‖

Play on the G tone bar while he draws.

Tune (C & G).

Play recordings of music to the child for him to draw and encourage him to use different colours to describe a variety of moods of the music.
    Repeat the music several times so the child can add to the symbols with more colours and build up a pattern for it.

Tune (C & G).

Follow-on Activities

1   Play recordings of music and encourage the child to draw and colour pictures of it. Let him draw and colour just as he likes, not necessarily using rhythmograms.

2   Find a variety of articles that are 'rubbish' and will make the sound of G. Make up 'Question and answer' tunes for a 'Junk Serenade'.

3   Play Musical Chairs. Explain to the child that he should run round and round all the time you play on the G tone bar, but as soon as you play on the C tone bar he must sit down on the nearest chair.

4   Play Statues. Starting at one end of the room, the child can run and walk forward while you play on G, but as soon as you play C he must 'freeze' on the spot. If he moves at all he must go back to the beginning. When he reaches the other end of the room a toffee is a suitable reward. This game helps develop self control.

Step 33   Further work on the piano

A great deal of repetition is needed before a sound is thoroughly learnt.

Access to a piano extends the range of sounds for the child to learn.

Turn to Steps 15,16,17 and 18 and repeat using the sound G instead of C. This work should take at least four days.

Tune to C and G.

Remind the child that the piano keyboard is made up of groups of two and three black notes.

Show the child the note G which is the second white note of the group around three black notes.

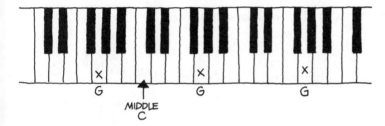

Tune to G only.

Ask the child to find all the Gs on the piano.

Tune to G only.

Ask the child to play the G which is to the right of middle C.

Tune to C and G.

Remind the child that moving 'up' the piano is moving to the right.

Ask the child to play the first G up from the Middle C. Explain that we sometimes use the words 'first G above Middle C' instead of 'first G up from Middle C'.

Explain that moving to the left of Middle C is going 'down' the piano, so those notes down from Middle C are 'below' Middle C.

Ask the child to play the Cs and Gs up from or above and then down from or below Middle C, in random order.

Tune (C & G).

In working through these activities, the greatest skill is the greatest amount of repetition that can be arranged without boring the child, *not* in covering the steps quickly.

Step 34 More discriminating between pitches

More haste, less speed. Ideally it should have taken about six months to reach this stage. Continual and massive repetition over a long period is needed for the development of auditory memory.

Many of the forty or so speech sounds that must be learnt for language are very close together in pitch. The xylophone, 'rubbish' and environmental sounds are used to help develop the fine discrimination needed.

Turn to Steps 20 and 21. Repeat these on the note G.

Tune to C and G.

Explore the rubbish for junk that can produce the sound of G – any G not just the one above Middle C.

Play 'Question and Answer' tunes on all the junk instruments and tape record them.

Tune (C & G).

Tape-record environmental sounds and sort out those which are tuned
to G.

Tune (C & G).

Compose a 'Junk Symphony in G' with the tape-recorded questions and answers on junk instruments, followed by as many environmental sounds on G as you could find, finishing off with the questions and answers on junk instruments again. Make sure the very last question and answer is on a junk instrument making the sound of middle C, to let everyone know the piece has finished; coming home to Doh at the end of a piece of music is like putting a full stop at the end of a sentence.

Discriminating between pitched sounds is the basis of spelling accurately.

Follow-on Activities
1   Introduce G to the family or class as the sound that means 'stand up'. Use it at the end of meals as a signal that the whole family may stand up and leave the table.

2   Continue with some rhythmograms on G. The child cannot practice these on his own.

3   Take the child to a playground, funfair or even on a day trip to a holiday camp. Let him have plenty of fun with swings, slides, roundabouts and see-saws. This experience is all valuable for developing the understanding needed for some of the future activities and for the collection of vocabulary.

4   Don't forget to keep adding to the picture dictionary collection.

5   Listen to 'Peter and the Wolf' again. Try to make up a story with sound illustrations of each of the characters.

Step 35   Introducing the Humpty family to 'Soh'

Symbolising a sound aids the learning of it.

Tune (C & G throughout this step).

Find your two-rung ladder and remind the child that the bottom run 'Doh' was the first step on the musical ladder, and that the middle rung was the fifth step on the musical ladder. Tell him the name of this middle rung is 'Soh'.

Take the xylophone to the stairs and ask the child to sing 'Doh' when he stands on the first step and 'Soh' when he stands on the fifth.

Tune.

Using the cut-out or model Humpty family, ask the child to introduce them all to the Soh rung of the ladder, singing as he does so;
    Mr Humpty sings Soh,
    Mrs Humpty sings Soh-oh,
    Mrs Humpty with baby Humpty on her back sings Soh-oh-oh,
    Granny Humpty sings Soh-oh-oh-oh.

Tune.

Ask the child to draw a separate ladder for each member of the family and, as you play and sing their sound, draw them sitting on the Soh rung.

Tune.

Suggest to the child that the Humpty family might all like to sit together on one fence instead of on separate ladders, though they will need to use one of the ladders to climb up.
    Ask him to draw a two 'rung' fence and sing as he sits each member of the Humpty family on it.

Tune.

Help the child to make a paper aeroplane.

Ask him to take off, fly and land it. As the plane starts moving along the ground, play on the C tone bar. When it takes off and as it flies around, play on the G tone bar. As it comes in to land return to playing on the C tone bar.

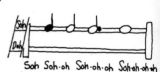

Soh   Soh-oh   Soh-oh-oh   Soh-oh-oh-oh

Tune.

Ask the child to listen carefully to your playing the xylophone. Explain that you will start playing on C and he must taxi along the runway until you start playing on G when he must take off and fly. When he hears you return to C again he must come in and land. Make sure he cannot see which tone bar you are playing, but uses his hearing.

While a child can hear the difference between two pitched sounds, then he is learning the sound ingredients of language. Don't forget however that this ability is affected by catarrhal colds on some days. Keep the record book carefully.

Step 36 Relating high and low

The ability to relate arises from previously-learnt experiences.

The swing is a very useful way of learning to relate high and low. Taking the xylophone (or tape recorded sounds of C and G) along to the playground helps to ensure that meaning is developed alongside the learning of the sounds.

Tune before leaving home. (C & G).

At the playground, let the child sit on a swing and practice swinging up and down. Ask him to look at everything round him to ensure that he is using his eyes.

Encourage him to sing 'Soh' as he swings up and 'Doh' as he comes down. Vary this with:
 Swing high (sung on Soh)
 Swing low (sung on Doh)

Tune (C & G).

Either in the playground or on returning home, sing, act and play the following song:

1 Stand up for Soh, (stand, play and sing on G)
 Sit down for Doh, (sit, play and sing on C)
 Soh-oh-oh-oh, (stand, play and sing on G)
 Doh-oh-oh-oh. (sit, play and sing on C)

2 Jump for soh
 Sit down for Doh
 Soh-oh-oh-oh
 Doh-oh-oh-oh

3 Hop for Soh, sit down for Doh etc.

4 March for Soh, etc.

5 Walk for Soh, etc.

6 Run for Soh, etc.

7   Skip for Soh, etc.

8   Crawl for Soh, etc.

Tune (C & G).

Meaningless sounds are not easily remembered.

Follow-on Activity
Play Hunt the Toffee, with the toffee at floor level if the sound
played is C, or off the floor if the sound is G. Otherwise the game
is the same.

Step 37   More work on G

The aim is to move on as slowly as possible.

Turn to steps 7, 8, 9, 10 and 12 and repeat all the activities on the
note G. This should take at least five days.

Make some more cards for the revision games 'Musical Parcel'
and 'Musical Snap' of all the sound making activities in steps 25
to 37, old as well as new. You might like to check the new
activities with the Stage Two Test Card in Step 38.

Play the games as in Step 22 and record any difficulties in the
record book.

G must be learnt as thoroughly as C before moving on.

Step 38   The second Test

The Stage Two Practice/Test card should now contain activities from Steps 5, 8-10, 12, 15-18, 20 and 21 which have been carried out on the note G, as well as the following new activities from steps 25 to 37:–

Date	Activity	Daily Practice							Test Passed
	Tuning of Mr. Humpty to 'C'								
	Tuning of Mrs. Humpty to 'C'								
	Mr. Humpty singing 'Doh'								
	Mrs. Humpty singing 'Doh-oh'								
	Mrs. Humpty with baby on her back sings 'Doh-oh-oh'								
	Grandma Humpty sings 'Doh-oh-oh-oh'								
	Play and sing 'C' touching toes, then 'G' touching middles before returning to touch toes and sing 'C' again								
	Searching out sounds of 'ff'								
	Play sound of sign ff								
	Play sound of sign f								
	Play sound of sign pp								
	Play sound of sign p								
	Play sound of >								
	Play sound of <								
	Find 'G's' on the piano and tune voice to piano 'G' above middle 'C'								
	Mr. Humpty sings 'Soh'								
	Mrs. Humpty sings 'Soh-oh'								
	Mrs. Humpty with baby on her back sings 'Soh-oh-oh'								
	Grandma Humpty sings 'Soh-oh-oh'								

Proceed with the testing as for Stage One (Step 23). When the child has successfully passed all the tests, award a Stage Two proficiency badge, deciding between you which motif to use.
   Pass on to Stage Three.

STAGE THREE

Step 39 Introducing E

The learning sandwich requires old work to be repeated for a short time daily while tackling new work, so make sure the daily practice is done and the practice card kept up to date.

Tune to C and G.

Explain to the child that you are now going to add the third step E to the musical ladder. Ask him to replace all the tone bars between Middle C and G on the xylophone.

Play up the musical ladder, C,D,E,F,G.

Ask the child to play C and hum in tune to it.

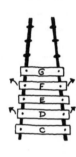

to play D and hum in tune to it, then lift it off the xylophone.

to play E, hum in tune to it but leave it on the xylophone.

to play F, hum in tune to it, then lift it off the xylophone.

to play G, hum in tune to it and leave it on the xylophone.

Point out that the three tone bars left on the xylophone are C, E and G and that E is the new tone bar.

Tune your voices to E.

Ask the child to make another picture ladder with three rungs looking like the xylophone, the new rung half way between Doh and Soh, just as E is half way between C and G. This new rung is called 'Me'.

Soh
Me
Doh

Mr Humpty sings 'Me'   Mrs Humpty sings 'Me'   Mrs Humpty with baby sings 'Me'   Granny Humpty sings 'Me'

Ask the child to introduce the Humpty family to the new rung of the ladder, singing their sound on the new rung.

Tune your voices to E.

Step 40   More work on E

More haste less speed. Many, many repetitions of a note are necessary for thorough learning.

Repeat Steps 5, 7 – 10, 12, 15 – 18, 20 and 21 on the note E to the sound Me.

Do not take more than one step a day; ideally provide a variety of approaches to make it possible to repeat a step for several days, but do not allow boredom to creep in.

Tune your voices to C, E and G.

Ask the child to act and sing 'We touch our knees for Me' while you play on E.

Tune to C, E and G.

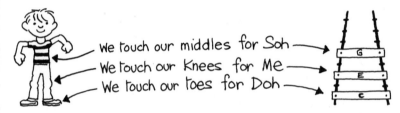

We touch our middles for Soh ⟶ G
We touch our Knees for Me ⟶ E
We touch our toes for Doh ⟶ C

Ask the child to practise singing and touching each of the three parts of his 'musical body' while you play the appropriate notes.

Tune to C, E and G.

Ask the child to make another fence, this time with three rungs, just like the ladder.

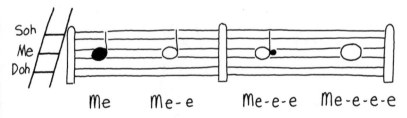

Soh
Me
Doh

me   me-e   me-e-e   me-e-e-e

Ask him to sit all the Humpty family on the E rung of the fence, play and sing their sounds.

Tune to C, E and G.

At the piano keyboard, ask the child to point to all the groups of two black notes.

Show him E, which is the right hand white note (facing the piano) of each group round the two black notes, half way between C and G.

Tune to E only.

Let the child find all the Es on the piano.

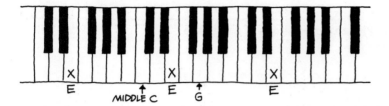

Ask him to find the E which is nearest the middle of the piano, play and hum it.

Tune to C, E and G.

Follow-on Activities
1   Add all the activities on the new note E or Me to the practice test card.

2   Before moving on to the next step, visit a children's playground so the child can get some experience of playing on a see-saw.

Step 41   Tunes to play, act and sing on one or two notes

Tune to C, E and G.

Busy Me
You play on E while the child sings and acts:–

Me, Me, busy Me
I tap my knees
When I sing Me
Me, Me, Me, Me.

Tune (C, E, G).

The See-Saw
Play the sounds to sing and teach the child the words while sitting on the see-saw.

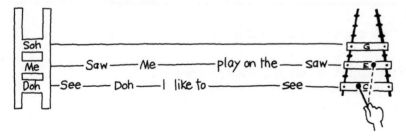

Tune (C, E, G).

The Cuckoo Song

Cuck - oo   Cuck - oo   Soh   Me   Soh   Me

Ask the child to take the whole Humpty family to hear the Cuckoo.

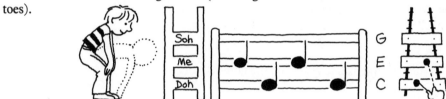

Soh Me   Soh-oh Me-e   Soh-oh-oh Me-e-e   Soh-oh-oh-oh Me-e-e-e

Tune (C, E, G).

Ding Dong, Ding Dong

When the child can play and sing 'Me–Doh' correctly, teach him the words and ask him to sing and act (touching his knees and toes).

Ding	Dong	Ding	Dong
Bells are	Singing	all day	long
Me	Doh	Me	Doh
Ding	Dong	Ding	Dong

Tune (C, E, G)

This old Man

Ask the child to hold up the appropriate number of fingers for each verse.

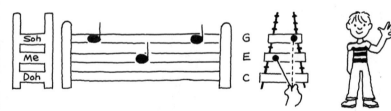

1	This	old	man
	He	played	one
2	This	old	man
	He	played	two
3	This	old	man
	He	played	three
4	This	old	man
	He	played	four
5	This	old	man
	He	played	five

Tune (C, E, G).

Keep it fun – variety of approach assists this. A bored child will not learn.

Jack in the Box

Ask the child to jump in time to his singing. Always sing the names of the rungs as well as the words.

Tune (C, E, G).

Turn to steps 31 and 32 and repeat on the note E to the sound Me.

Tune (C, E, G).

Skip to My Lou
Remember to sing both the names of the rungs and the words.

Tune (C, E, G).

The Mulberry Bush

Tune (C, E, G).

Loo-by Lou.

Test the learning of this stage, using the practice/test card, before moving on to Stage Four.

STAGE FOUR

Step 43   Introducing the sound A

Keep up the practice and the test card.

Tune (C, E, G).

Ask the child to put all the tone bars on the xylophone, and play right up the musical ladder.

Ask the child to prepare the xylophone for learning the new note (as below) starting at the bottom with C and working upwards to the new note.

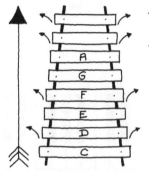

} Remove these notes without humming them

The new note A. Play, Hum and leave on the xylophone
Play and sing Soh and leave on the xylophone
Play and hum and lift off the xylophone
Play and sing Me and leave on the xylophone
Play and hum and lift off the xylophone
Play and sing Doh and leave on the xylophone

Point out that the four tone bars left on the xylophone are C, E, G and A, and that A is the new tone bar.
   Play and hum up and down the xylophone.

Tune your voices to A.

Ask the child to draw a four-rung ladder, with the new rung the same distance above Soh as Doh, Me and Soh are apart.

Explain to the child that for the first time, the new sound does not sit on a rung of the ladder, but swings in between the rungs. The new sound A swings from the fourth rung in the space just above Soh called Lah.

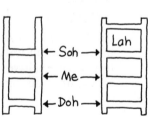

Ask the child to let the whole Humpty family swing from the fourth rung, singing their sounds as they swing in the space.

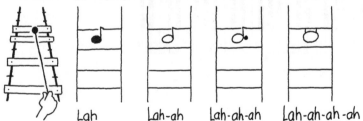

Lah   Lah-ah   Lah-ah-ah   Lah-ah-ah-ah

Visit the children's playground and let the child swing from a climbing frame just as the new sound swings on the ladder.

Tune to A.

Step 44   More work on A

More haste, less speed!

Repeat Steps 5, 7 – 10, 12, 15 – 18, 20, 21, 31 & 32 on the note A to the sound Lah. Do not take more than one step a day.

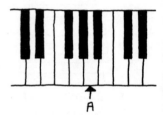

Tune to C, E, G and A.

Ask the child to add 'touching his shoulders to Lah' to his musical body while you play on A.

Ask him to practice touching all the parts of his musical body as you play

Tune (C, E, G, A).

At the piano, ask the child to point to all the groups of three black notes.

Show him A which is the white note to the right of the second black note in each group of three.

Tune to A.

Ask the child to find all the As on the piano. He should discover that A is the first note at the bottom of the piano (or so it is on most pianos).

Tune to A.

Ask the child to say his alphabet. Explain that the musical alphabet is very short, just A B C D E F G. When it is finished we start again at A – A B C D E F G, A B C D E F G, A B C D E etc.

Ask the child to find the very first or bottom A on the piano and then say the musical alphabet as he plays up the white notes one by one. (If you have easy access to a piano get him to do this several times during the day.)

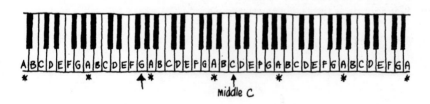

Ask the child to count up from A to G twice and play this second G on the piano. He should soon be able to go to the piano and play the second G without hesitating. This will be very useful later on.

Tune to A.

Follow-on Activities

1   Explain to the child that all the instruments of the orchestra tune to the sound A.

Watch and listen for the Orchestra to tune before and during Radio and television concerts, and join in by playing the A tone bar of the xylophone. (You may have to listen very carefully for the orchestra tuning, as often the announcer is speaking at the same time. However when there is a concerto for a solo instrument other than a piano, the soloist will usually tune to the orchestral oboe on the platform just before starting to play.)

Watching instruments being played while listening to them will develop the child's ability to recognise their various tonal qualities.

Television is particularly useful for this, as it shows close-ups of the instruments and the child can learn to mime the actions of playing them.

Step 45   Songs for singing and playing using notes C, E, G and A

Tune the voice to C, E, G and A, both before starting each song and whenever necessary during the learning session.

When the child has played and sung each song,

1   Encourage him to learn it from memory to the names of the sounds e.g. Soh-oh Me Lah Soh-oh and so on, before he uses the word.

2   Ask him to draw a four rung fence and draw in the Humptys while singing the song from memory.

Rain, Rain Go Away

Soh-oh Me-e Soh Soh Me-e Soh Soh Me   Lah Soh Soh Me-e
Rain Rain go a....way, Come A...gain A......no..ther Day

Lucy Locket

Soh Soh Lah Lah Soh Soh Me Me Soh Soh Lah Lah Soh-oh Me-e
Lu..cy Lo...cket lost her po..cket, Ki..tty Fi..sher found it.

Ring a Ring a Roses

Bye Baby Bunting

Traffic Lights

Test the learning of Stage Four before moving on.

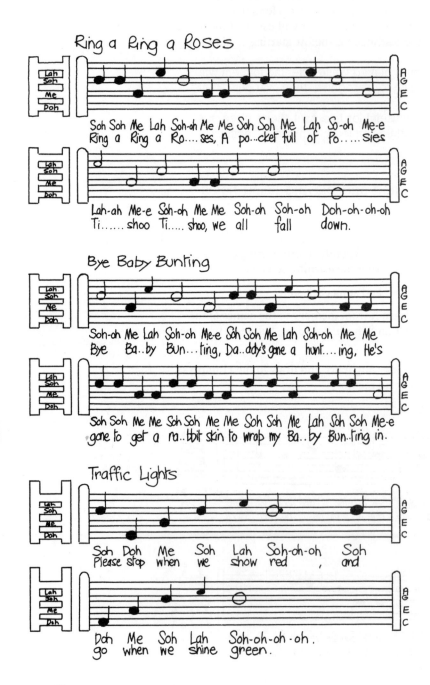

78

STAGE FIVE

Step 46 Introducing Top C

Keep up practice and test card.

Tune (C, E, G, A)

Ask the child to put all the tone bars on the xylophone and to play right up the musical ladder, humming each note as he plays.

Starting at the bottom with C, ask the child to prepare the xylophone for learning the new note.

The new note, Top C. Play hum and leave on.
Play, hum and take off.
Play, sing Lah and leave on
Play, Sing Soh and leave on
Play, hum and take off.
Play, Sing Me and leave on
Play, hum and take off
Play, sing Doh and leave on.

Point out that the new note is also a C and is called Top C. Sometimes it is written C′ to distinguish it from Middle C.

Tune your voices to Top C (C′).

Ask the child to draw a ladder with another rung above the rest, so it now has five.
   Explain that Top C swings in the space between the fourth and fifth rungs which is called Top Doh, sometimes written Doh′.

Tune to top C.

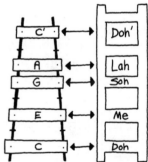

Ask the child to draw a five-runged fence and to draw all the Humpty family swinging in the top C space. Ask him to sing their sounds as he draws them while you play on the xylophone.

Doh   Doh-oh   Doh-oh-oh   Doh-oh-oh-oh

Step 47 More Work on Top C

Keep it fun!

Repeat all the Steps 5, 7 – 10, 12, 15 – 18, 20, 21, 31 and 32 on the note C' (Top C) to the sound of Doh'. Do not rush them.

Tune (C, E, G, A and C').

Ask the child to practice touching all the parts of his musical body as he sings and you play, adding 'We stretch up for top Doh' for top C.

Tune (C, E, G, A, C').

At the piano, ask the child to find Top C, which is the first C above Middle C, and play and hum the sound.

Add the following song to your repertoire.

Ding Dong Bell

Doh Soh Doh Doh Doh Soh Soh Doh   Me Doh Doh Me Me Me Doh Doh Me
Ding Dong Bell Puss..y's in the well, Who put him in, Litt..le John..ny Flinn

Doh Soh Soh Doh Doh Doh Soh Soh   Doh
Who pulled him out Litt..le John..ny Stout

Ask the child to play and practise each of the songs you have learnt so far on the piano.

Test the learning of Stage Five before moving on.

STAGE SIX

Step 48 Introducing D

Tune (C, E, G, A, C′).

With the tone bars C, E, G, A and C′ on the xylophone, ask the child to play and sing all the sounds learnt so far.

Ask the child to find the tone bar marked D which fits between Middle C and E on the xylophone. This is the new note.

Tune your voices to D.

Explain that D swings in the space between Doh and Me on the ladder, which is called Ray.

Ask the child to draw and sing all the Humpty family swinging in the D space on the five rung fence.

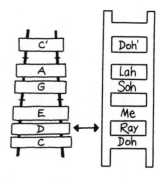

Ray   Ray-ay   Ray-ay-ay   Ray-ay-ay-ay

Tune to D.

At the piano, ask the child to find all the Ds, which are the white notes in the middle of each group of two black notes. Ask the child to hum the D on the xylophone each time he plays a D on the piano.

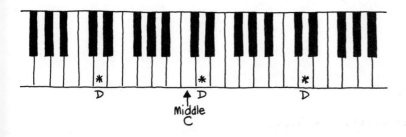

Step 49 More work on D

Repeat Steps 5, 7 – 10, 12, 15 – 18, 20, 21, 31 & 32 on the note D to the sound Ray.

Tune to C, E, G, A, C' and D.

Ask the child to sing, touching all the parts of the musical body he has learnt while you play the xylophone or piano.

Ask him which part he thinks should represent Ray and to act and sing 'We touch our shins for Ray'.

Ask the child to stretch up and down from his toes to each part of his musical body in turn, first humming then singing each sound as he does so while you play . . .

Touch toes, hum C, sing Doh . . . Touch shins, hum D, sing Ray
Touch toes, hum C, sing Doh . . . Touch knees, hum E, sing Me
Touch toes, hum C, sing Doh . . . Touch middle, hum G, sing Soh
Touch toes, hum C, sing Doh . . . Touch shoulders, hum A, sing Lah
Touch toes, hum C, sing Doh . . . Touch stretch up, hum C, sing Doh'

Try playing the sounds in random order while the child listens with closed eyes and then touches the correct part of his musical body.

Tune (C, E, G, A, C' and D).

Step 50   Towards musical notation

Tune (C, D, E, G, A, C' through Steps 50 & 51).

Ask the child to play and sing the following tune.

The Skaters Waltz

Stretch up = Doh'

Shoulders = Lah

Middle = Soh

Knees = Me

Shins = Ray

Toes = Doh

Doh Ray Me Soh-oh-oh Me Ray Doh Soh-oh-oh

Turn to Step 20. Remind the child how he emphasised the first count when counting '1, 2, 3' for the dance called the waltz. Explain that we can put fencing posts along the five-rung fence to show that the first sound of the next bit of fence should be emphasised. As the tune you have just played is a waltz, the posts should go after every third count and it will look like this:

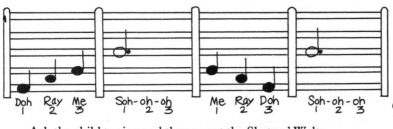

Doh Ray Me   Soh- oh- oh   Me Ray Doh   Soh- oh- oh
1   2   3   1   2   3   1   2   3   1   2   3

Ask the child to sing and then count the Skaters' Waltz, emphasising the first sound/count after each fence post. You play for him, slightly emphasising the first sound with him.

Tune.

Ask the child to accompany himself as he sings or counts, emphasising the first sound or count after the fence post in both his voice and on the xylophone. Explain that the sounds are sung or played slightly louder to give the feeling of what is called the beat of the music.

Tune.

Ask the child to play sing and count the following tune:

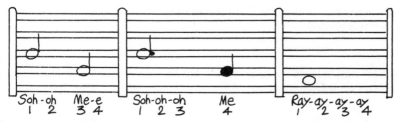

Soh - oh   Me-e   Soh-oh-oh   Me   Ray-ay-ay-ay
1   2   3   4   1   2   3   4   1   2   3   4

Step 51   A further step towards musical notation

In this, and the remaining steps, the fence is modified in order to
resemble more closely conventional musical notation.

Tune.

Explain to the child that the grass in the field has now grown so
long that it is covering up the bottom rung of the fence. This rung
will now only be visible when something is sitting on it. This
means that The Skaters' Waltz will look like this:

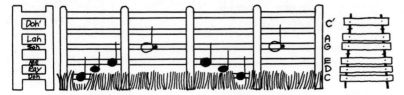

Ask the child to play and sing The Skaters' Waltz, remembering
to emphasise the first sound after each fence post.

Ask the child to draw The Skaters' Waltz with the grass growing
over the bottom rung.

Tune.

Au Clair de la Lune
Ask the child to sing, play and act, by touching the appropriate
parts of his musical body, this tune.

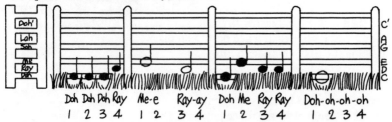

Tune.

Ask the child to sing the tune again, marching round the room in
time to it. Remind him to accent the first sound after each fence
post.

Tune.

Ask the child to draw the tune, reminding him that you can only
see the bottom rung when it is needed.

Tune.

Tell the child that you want him to learn the tune so well that he
will be able to play, sing and act it from memory.

Tune.

I Can Play
Carry out all the same activities on this tune as with Au Clair de la
Lune, but explain that instead of drawing the grass all the time
the child should just use a dotted line to remind him of the unseen
C rung of the fence, only drawing the run itself when it is needed.

Test the learning of Stage Six before moving on.

STAGE SEVEN

Step 52   Introducing F

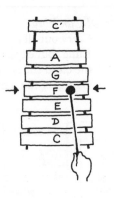

Tune.

With the C, D, E, G, A and C' tone bars on the xylophone, ask the child to play and sing all the sounds he has learnt so far.

Ask the child to find the tone bar marked F which fits between E and G on the xylophone. This is the new note.

Tune your voices to F.

Explain that F swings in the space between Me and Soh on the ladder and is called Fah.

Ask the child to draw and sing all the Humpty family swinging in the F space on the five rung fence. Remind him that the grass has grown over the C rung so to draw it as a dotted line.

Tune to F.

Explain that although this new sound F does not need a new rung, eventually you will be learning to sing another F a little way above top C' and this has a new rung right at the top of the ladder or fence and will be called top F or F'.

Ask the child to draw a new fence with a new top rung. It should have five rungs showing, and the C rung represented by a dotted line.

Fah   Fah-ah   Fah-ah-ah   Fah-ah-ah-ah

Tune to F.

At the piano, ask the child to find all the Fs which are the white notes just to the left of each group of three black notes.

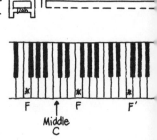

Ask him to find the F nearest middle C, play it and tune his voice to it.

Ask him to find the next F up the piano, which is top F. This is almost certainly too high for the child to sing, but if you can, sing it (if not, just play it) while the child draws the Humpty family sitting on this top rung.

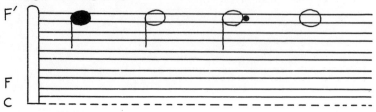

Step 53   More work on F

Repeat all the Steps 5, 7 – 10, 12, 15 – 18, 20, 21, 31 and 32 on F to the sound Fah.

Stretch up = Doh'
Shoulders = Lah
Middle = Soh
Thighs = Fah
Knees = Me
Shins = Ray
Toes = Doh

Tune (C, D, E, G, A, C' and F through Steps 53 and 54).

Ask the child to sing and touch all the parts of his musical body so far learnt.

Add 'We touch our thighs for Fah' to the list.

Tune.

Ask the child to touch and sing backwards and forward from his toes to all the other parts of his musical body: Doh – Ray, Doh – Me, Doh – Fah and so on to Doh – Doh'.

Tune.

Three Blind Mice
Ask the child to play, sing the sounds, count and touch the appropriate parts of his musical body to this tune.

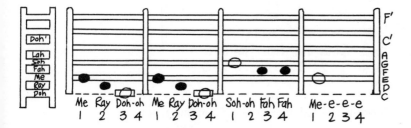

Me Ray Doh-oh Me Ray Doh-oh Soh-oh Fah Fah Me-e-e-e
1   2   3 4   1   2   3 4   1   2   3   4   1   2 3 4

Ask the child if he recognises the tune and let him sing the words.

Tune.

Ask the child to draw the tune.

Explain that you are now going to teach him a quicker way to draw this and all the other tunes he has learnt which will also help him to know just how to sing and play them.

Demonstrate each stage to the child and let him copy what you have done.

Explain that instead of drawing each rung of the fence using two lines, to draw it as only one line would be much quicker.

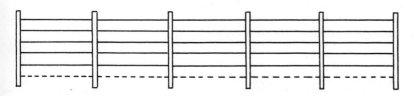

87

Tune

Explain that although you still need a strong fence post at each
end to hold the new fence up, the fence posts that come in the
middle (to show that you have to accent the next count) can also
be drawn as single lines. Tell him that these are called 'bar lines'
in music.

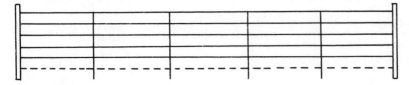

Tune.

Explain that each section of fence between the fence posts or bar
lines is called a 'bar' of music. Most pieces of music have the same
number of counts or beats in each bar and you can show how
many this is by putting a number at the beginning. Three Blind
Mice has four counts to a bar, so it now looks like this:

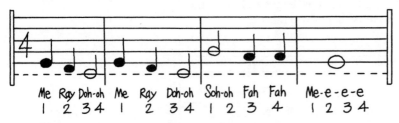

Me Ray Doh-oh Me   Ray Doh-oh Soh-oh Fah Fah   Me-e-e-e
1   2 34   1   2   34   1 2 3   4   1 2 3 4

Tune.

Suggest that instead of drawing a dotted line to remind you that
middle C has a line which you cannot always see, you only draw a
little line when it is needed:–

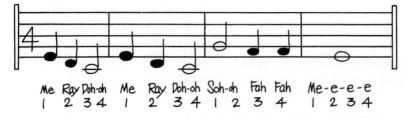

Me Ray Doh-oh Me   Ray Doh-oh Soh-oh Fah Fah   Me-e-e-e
1   2 34   1   2   3 4   1 2   3   4   1 2 3 4

Tune.

Ask the child to draw The Skaters' Waltz the new way (see Steps
50 and 51).

Ask the child to draw 'Au Clair de la Lune' and 'I Can Play' (from
memory if he is able) the new way. Do not forget to put the
number representing the right number of counts in each bar, at
the beginning.

A check for the three tunes will be found on page 95.

Step 54 The sound of silence

Tune.

Remind the child of the action to be taken for the rest sign (see Step 27).

Ask the child to play, sing and act (by touching the appropriate parts of his musical body) the next song several times until he can repeat the singing and action from memory.

Join in the Game

Soh		Soh	Lah	Soh	Fah	Me	Ray	Doh		Soh	Doh	
3		I	2	3	I	2	3	I	2	3	I	2

Tune.

Ask the child to draw the notes from memory.

Tune.

Ask the child to learn the words, carrying out the actions specified on the last two notes.

Verse 1.

Let	ev' -- ry	one	clap	hands	with me	(clap,clap)
It's	ea --- sy	as	ea---- sy	can	be	(clap,clap)
Let	ev' -- ry	one	join in	the	game	(clap,clap)
You'll	find that	it's	al ---- ways	the	same	(clap,clap

Verse 2. Let everyone whistle with me (whistle, whistle)

Verse 3. Let everyone tap feet with me (tap, tap)

Verse 4. Let everyone blink eyes with me (blink, blink)

Tune.

Remind the child where to find C, D, E, F, G, A and C' on the piano as separate notes.

Ask him to play all the tunes in Steps 50, 51, 53 as well as this one, on the piano.

Test the learning of Stage Seven before moving on.

STAGE EIGHT

Step 55   Introducing B

Tune (C, D, E, F, G, A, C′).

Tell the child there is only one more note to learn on the musical ladder. The note is B and is between A and top C on the xylophone.

Ask the child to place all the tone bars on the xylophone and tune his voice to B.

B, which is called Te, sits on the rung between Lah and Doh′ on the ladder.

Ask the child to draw all the Humpty family on the B rung of the fence and sing their sounds.

Tune to B.

Ask the child to find all the Bs on the piano, which are the white notes to the right of each group of three black notes.

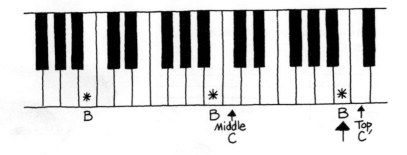

Find the B which is just below C′ on the piano and tune your voices to it.

Ask the child to play and hum all the white notes he has learnt from middle C up to top C. Tell him that this row of notes, C D E F G A B C′, is called a scale′ of C.

Add 'We touch our head for Te'·to the musical body.

Ask the child to sing and touch backwards and forwards from his toes to all the other parts of his musical body in turn: Doh – Ray, Doh – Me, Doh – Fah and so on.

Tune to B.

Step 56 More work on B

Repeat Steps 5, 7 – 10, 12, 15 – 18, 20, 21, 31 & 32 on B to the sound Te.

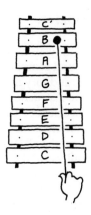

Tune to the whole scale of C.

Ask the child to play, sing, count, act, memorise and draw the following song:–

One Elephant

Tune to the scale of C.

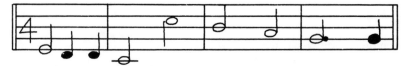

Me-e	Ray	Ray	Doh-oh	Doh-oh'	Te-e	Lah-ah	Soh-oh-oh	Soh
1 2 3 4	1 2 3 4	1 2 3 4	1 2 3 4
One	e..l..e	phant	went	out	to		play	up-

Soh-oh	Doh-oh	Fah-ah	Me-e	Me-e	Ray-ay	Doh-oh-oh-oh
1 2 3 4	1 2 3 4	1 2 3 4	1 2 3 4
on	a	spi.....	der's	web	one	day.

Conclusion

With your help, your child will by now have explored all the sound components of language, and will have begun to establish an auditory memory – provided, of course, that you have followed the instructions carefully, that any problems showing up in the record book have been attended to, and that the child has had sufficient experience at every stage. He should be capable of learning all speech sounds, which means he will be able to make full use of the visual symbols that represent them as he learns to read, write and spell.

As a bonus he will have reached the threshold of musical literacy. He will have learnt all the notes of the scale of C, and will be able to write them down from middle C upwards:

In conventional notation that might be written:

𝄞 is called the treble clef, and indicates that the fence of music (or 'stave') is above middle C.

$\frac{4}{4}$ indicates that there are four counts (or beats) in each bar.

The same scale, written to be played lower down the piano, might look like this:

↑
This note is also middle C.

𝄢 is called the bass clef, and indicates that the fence or stave is below middle C.

In piano music the staves are joined together, the treble usually being played by the right, the bass by the left hand.

If your child looks at the opening bars of Mozart's *Minuet in F*:

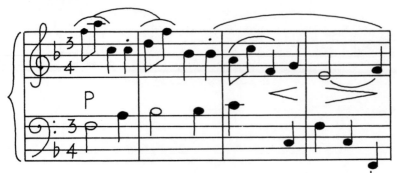

he will see many things he will recognise – notes written like ♩ and 𝅝 , and signs showing how loud or soft to play

(< >), which he learnt in Step 31.

There are also things he hasn't yet learnt – notes written ♫ (each of the pair being half as long as ♩); the flat sign ♭ (which in this piece sits on B, and means that, throughout the piece, instead of playing B on the piano you are to play the black note immediately below it – the B flat); and signs like ⁴⁄₄ and (which show how to phrase the music). But you can see he is not really very far away from reading and playing conventional music.

You can provide essential reinforcement and development of his present learning by continuing his music education with the help of a sympathetic teacher, who will take into account what he already knows.

The Skater's Waltz

Au Clair de la Lune

I Can Play